KU-318-914

M . USAMA

ICT Matters 1

Liz Hankin • David Sutton • David Dunn

www.heinemann.co.uk
✓ Free online support
✓ Useful weblinks
✓ 24 hour online orde

01865 8880

Heinemann is an imprint of Pearson Education Limited, a company incorporated in England and Wales, having its registered office at Edinburgh Gate, Harlow, Essex, CM20 2JE. Registered company number: 872828

Heinemann is a registered trademark of Pearson Education Limited

© Liz Hankin, David Sutton, David Dunn, 2003

First published 2003

11
10 9 8

British Library Cataloguing in Publication Data is available from the British Library on request.

ISBN: 978 0 435108 33 5
Expresscode 8395P

Copyright notice

All rights reserved. No part of this publication may be reproduced in any form or by any means (including photocopying or storing it in any medium by electronic means and whether or not transiently or incidentally to some other use of this publication) without the written permission of the copyright owner, except in accordance with the provisions of the Copyright, Designs and Patents Act 1988 or under the terms of a licence issued by the Copyright Licensing Agency, 90 Tottenham Court Road, London W1T 4LP. Applications for the copyright owner's permission should be addressed to the publisher.

Designed by Wooden Ark Studio
Produced by Kamae Design, Oxford

Original illustrations © Harcourt Education Limited 2003
Illustrated by Kamae Design pp. 93, 111, 148, 149 and 157, Phil Healey pp. 7, 14, 38, 112, 146 and 151, Tim Kahane pp. iv, 1, 4, 5, 12, 15, 17, 20, 36, 42, 44, 53, 60, 64, 82, 92, 94, 113, 117, 124, 128, 133, 135, 141 and 150, Steve Lach pp. 23 and 72, Colin Mier pp. 12, 32, 85 and 144, Melanie Sharpe pp. 34, 43, 102, 133 and 149, p151 Louise Curphey
Cover design by Hicksdesign
Printed in China (SWTC/08)

on; Corbis; p23
33, 35 John
p52 Getty; Trevor
p69 Peter Morris;
ies; p135 Alamy /
ng-Wolff; p138
gy; p139 SPL; p140
17 Alamy / Phototake;
7 Corbis; p164 Alamy.

Acknowledgements

Every effort has been made to contact copyright holders of material reproduced in this book. Any omissions will be rectified in subsequent printings if notice is given to the publishers.

P7 Oxfam Fairtrade Coffee advert reproduced with the kind permission of Oxfam GB; Extract from 'Geographer's A–Z Street Atlas of Lincoln & District'. Reprinted with the kind permission of Geographer's A–Z Map Company Limited and Ordnance Survey; p39 Screengrab from www.wwf.org.uk reproduced with kind permission of WWF-UK; Screengrab from www.puffin.co.uk reproduced with the kind permission of Penguin Books UK; p40 Screengrab from www.google.com reproduced with the kind permission of Google USA; Screengrab from www.yahooligans.com reproduced with permission of Yahoo! Inc. © 2003 by Yahoo! Inc. YAHOO! and the YAHOO! logo are trademarks of Yahoo! Inc.; Screengrab from www.dogpile.co.uk reproduced with the kind permission of Infospace uk; p53 Screengrab from www.virginmobile.com/mobile reprinted with the kind permission of Virgin Mobile; p54 Two adverts from Clarks 'Life's One Long Catwalk' campaign. Reprinted with the kind permission of C & J Clark International Limited; Egg.com logo reproduced with the kind permission of Egg.com PR Team; Smile.co.uk logo reprinted with the kind permission of Smile Marketing; Goldfish logo reproduced with the kind permission of Centrica; p59 McDonald's Golden Arches logo reprinted with the kind permission of McDonalds; British Gas logo reprinted with the kind permission of British Gas Brand Management; IKEA logos reprinted with the kind permission of IKEA public relations; AA logo reprinted with the kind permission of AA Brand Communications; Hovis logo reproduced with the kind permission of British Bakeries; Penguin logo reprinted with the kind permission of Penguin UK; p62 J17 cover reprinted with the kind permission of Emap élan syndication; All Terrain Boarding, August 2003 Issue 14 cover reprinted with the kind permission of ATB Magazine; pp115, 118 Screengrab from www.prb.org, Graph Chart 2 'Northern Europe in Mid 2002' and Graph Chart 3 'Northern Europe in Mid 2002'. Reprinted with the kind permission of Population Reference Bureau, Washington, USA; Module 6 Screengrabs and commands from Logicator reproduced with the kind permission of Economatics; Control commands from Flowol reproduced with the kind permission of Rod Bowker, copyright owner of 'Flowol 2' by *Keep I.T. Easy (KITE)*. Flowol is distributed by Data Harvest; Screenshots reprinted with permission from Microsoft Corporation.

Introduction

Welcome to ICT Matters

This is the first of three books designed to help you develop all the ICT knowledge and skills you need during Key Stage 3. We hope that you will enjoy the books as well as learning a lot from them.

The following information will help you get the most out of this book, so it is worth spending a couple of minutes reading it.

This book has six Modules, each made up of a number of Units. Each unit contains information and tasks for you to do, either on your own, with a partner, or in a larger group.

For each module there is an Assignment which covers the same ground as the work you have been doing in the Module. You will be expected to work through this largely on your own.

At the end of each module there is a Skills help section. You can easily find these sections because they are printed on grey paper. They contain step-by-step instructions on how to use the software needed to do the tasks.

There are three different symbols within this book:

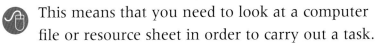 This means that you need to look at a computer file or resource sheet in order to carry out a task.

▶ *Skills help*

This tells you where to look in the Skills help section for help with a particular ICT skill.

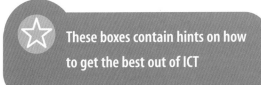 These boxes contain hints on how to get the best out of ICT

There are three types of tasks:

Red tasks will take you quite a long time to do and will need a lot of thought.

Green tasks are easier and should take less time.

Module tasks are like mini-projects which you work on throughout a module, gradually adding bits each lesson.

Hotlinks

Sometimes during a task you will need to look at a specific website. These are all listed on the Heinemann website and can be accessed by visiting www.heinemann.co.uk/hotlinks. When you get to that page, type in express code **8395P**. You can then select the website you need.

Building a portfolio

As you work through this course you will be building up a **portfolio**. This is a ring binder or folder in which you can keep printouts of your work as you go along. The portfolio is yours and you should use it to help you learn. If you make a mistake, write down what went wrong and what you could do differently next time. If you do something which works really well, highlight it so that you remember how to do it again, and tell your friends so that they can learn too!

At the end of each module there is an assignment to help your teacher assess your progress. Your work on the assignments will also go in your portfolio.

Jessie and her friends

Jessie has recently moved to a different school and met up with a group of new friends:

Jessie

Dara

Ramana

Sajid

Ben

They have decided to help each other by asking questions and sharing ideas. Look out for them as you work through the modules and tasks in this book.

ICT Matters e-tutor

You can also meet Jessie and her friends on the **ICT Matters e-tutor**. This is an electronic learning package, based on ICT Matters, which will help you develop your ICT skills. You can work your way through the skills at your own pace, or catch up with things you missed.

Contents

In this module you will be creating a presentation.

Before you start there are some skills and words that you will need to know.
Read about each skill in the boxes below and then decide which of the following
statements best describes how you feel about it:

A I am confident that I understand / can do this.
B I think I understand / can do this, but I would like to check.
C I definitely don't know how to do this and I need to learn.

Log on to the school network

Log on. This means the way in which you can access the school network. You will be given a **user name** and a **password**.

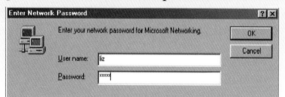

User name. You will be told this by your teacher. Remember it, as you can only get onto the network by typing it in.

Password. This is a special code that only you know. You will be told how many letters it can have. Decide on something easy to remember but something that others would not be able to guess.

Use a shared area to load and save work

Shared area. This is an area of space on the school network that has been set up so that you can load work from it and save work in it. When you are working on the school network you and your class will all use the same shared area for your work. Your teacher will tell you how to access the shared area.

Use the file names suggested by the school

File names. These are the names you give to documents that you save on the computer. The school may have its own rules about how to name files so that they can be easily found on the school network. If so, you should always use those rules. If your teacher lets you make up your own file names then choose something that will help you to remember what the file is about. For instance, if you have been writing a letter then the file name could be 'letter'. However, the rest of the class may have been writing letters, so make it special for you by using your initials or your nickname and then 'letter', for example 'jezletter.doc'.

Use presentation software

Presentation software. This allows you to create a set of screens called **slides** that can be shown through a computer.

Slides. These are like pages in a book. Each one can be different. You can have different colours and styles for the text. You can add images and sounds. You can move between the slides in the same way as you turn pages in a book.

Enter text into a presentation

Enter text. You usually enter text by typing in words using a keyboard. You can use different **fonts**.

Fonts. These are the types of letters used.

Insert pictures into a presentation

Pictures. On computers these are often called images. They can be **clip art**, pictures you have drawn, photographs or images from the Internet.

Clip art. This is a set of images that are ready for you to use. You can find them on the network. Your teacher will be able to show you how to access them.

Edit text and pictures

Edit. This means changing the way items look. You can enlarge, reduce, stretch, rotate or **crop** them.

Crop. This means cutting off part of an image using software.

Move text and pictures

Move. By clicking on an image to get **handles**, or **highlighting** text, you can move it or 'drag and drop' it to a new position.

Handles. When you click on an image, small squares appear, these are known as handles.

Highlighting. By clicking with the mouse and moving across words, you highlight the text.

Copy and paste text and pictures

Copy. By selecting an image or text you can make a **copy** of it.

Paste. Once you have copied something you can **paste** it to another place. You do not lose the original thing.

Create slides in a presentation

Create slides. This means the process of setting up the different screens for a presentation. The screens are the **slides**.

Use sound files

Sound files. These are computer files that contain sounds. They can be found in the Sound Gallery, recorded by you or taken from the Internet. Sounds are often used in presentations. Before they can be used they must be saved as sound files.

Print files

You will need to ask your leader to make sure that your computer is set up correctly to print.

Remember, always ask permission from your teacher before you print any document, as you will probaby be sharing a printer with lots of other people.

Task 1

1 Log on to the school network and go to the shared area. Find and open the file called **Resource 1 Mico's circus**. Save a version of it to your part of the shared area. Give it a new file name.

2 Enter the following text on Slide 4 after the heading: **Gasp in amazement as Mico's tiny team walk the high wire, race their bikes and call their friends on the telephone!** Change the font to Comic Sans 24pt.

3 Create a new slide at the beginning of the presentation and insert an image. Change the image if you want to.

4 When you are happy, copy the image. Paste it into each of the other slides. Change the image, if necessary, to fit.

5 Go back to the first slide. Insert a sound file from the Sound Gallery to go with the image on the slide.

6 Save your final version with a new file name (you could put 'v1' or 'version 1' at the end).

Unit 1.1
Putting in the content

What is a presentation?

A presentation is a way of communicating information and ideas to someone else. **Presentation software** combines text with colours, **images** and sounds into slides, which help to get a message across.

The people watching a presentation are called the **audience**. Sometimes a speaker talks to an audience and uses slides to emphasise main points. If there is no speaker then the slides must contain all the information.

Task 1

 Look at **Resource 1.1 My pets.**

1 Write down five things you learnt.

2 Write down five things you would like to know.

3 What does the presentation lead you to think about the subject and why?

Task 2

 Look at Resource **1.1 School information 1** and **Resource 1.1 School information 2.**

These presentations are both trying to communicate the same information.

1 What do you think the reason for presenting the information could be?

2 Which was more successful in communicating that message and why?

It is not enough just to give out information. It is important that the person who receives the message has understood it.

'What time does the train leave?'

'It says 3.30.'

'What, in the morning?!'

Purpose and audience

When making a presentation, a key thing to think about is the **purpose**:

- **Why** are you doing it?
- What is the key message you are trying to get across?
- Are you mainly trying to give information, or to entertain?

Another key thing is the intended audience:

- **Who** is going to be watching your presentation?
- How old are they?
- How well can they read?
- What do they already know about the subject?

Task 3

Think about one of the presentations you have watched.

1 What do you think was the purpose of the presentation?

2 Who do you think was the intended audience?

3 How could you change the content to make it more suitable for an audience of the parents of the children who will be coming to school next year?

A good presentation will	Things that make a bad presentation
Be easy to read	Misspelled words
Be easy to understand	Background pictures that make text difficult to read
Have a clear beginning, middle and end	Too much information on a slide
Take into account the needs of the intended audience	Fancy fonts in colours that are hard to read
	Anything which makes it hard for the intended audience to get the message!

Headings and bullet points

A **heading** at the top of each slide shows what the main subject is.

Bullet points make information easier to read. It is best to keep them short and simple, containing information about one thing. For example:

The people in my family

- My mum. Her name is Cathy and she looks after my brother and me.
- My dad. His name is Steve and he is a bus driver.
- My big brother Simon who is twelve. We fight all the time.
- Ross is our dog. He is a collie dog and he loves going for a walk.

Module Task

In this module you are going to create your own presentation. The purpose is to introduce yourself to the rest of your class. The audience will be the other members of your class.

a *Write down six different pieces of information about yourself that you want to include in your presentation, for example 'My family' or 'My hobbies'. These will be the headings at the top of the slides.*

b *Open PowerPoint in **Outline** view and enter your slide headings. Are they in the best order? If not use the **Slide Sorter** to change the order.*

c *Enter the content you want to put under each heading, using bullet points. Think about:*
- *what would others want to know about me?*
- *what would be useful to them?*
- *is the information in the right order?*
- *will they understand it?*

d *Print off your slides and save your work.*

 ## Skills help

Entering text in PowerPoint, page 27.

Using the **Slide Sorter** in PowerPoint, page 24.

Task 4

1 *Read through your presentation. Mark any improvements you want to make on the printout.*

2 *Think about what images you want to use in your presentation, for example images from the Internet, or cuttings from a magazine. Bring them to the next lesson.*

Unit 1.2
Using images

In this unit you will learn how images can be used to give information or add interest to a presentation. You will format images correctly and add them into your presentation using a scanner or camera.

Fitness for purpose

If an image is **fit for a purpose** it should be obvious why it was used. An image can take the place of words altogether, or it can make the meaning of words clearer.

Images can be used to:

- provide information you need

- make particular people look at them

From Oxfam's 'Make trade fair' campaign

- add extra impact

- provide a simplified version of an item

19 Grange Street, Chester

£125,000

* Two bedroom terrace * Reception Hallway * Lounge to rear * Dining Room * Kitchen * Utility * Landing * Two good sized bedrooms * Bathroom * Rear views over Cheshire countryside

Marketed by Brendon Property, 14 High Street, Chester. 01244 600 621

- provide an accurate version of an item

- teach you how to do something.

Task 1

*Look at **Resource 1.2 Images** and then complete **Resource 1.2 What's it for?***

For each image consider the following questions:

1 What is the purpose of the image?

2 Is it a good or bad choice?

3 Give reasons for your answers.

> ⭐ **It is important to make sure that images are saved in the right format for the job.**

Different kinds of image files

Images or graphics can be saved in different file formats.

This is a **bitmapped graphic** that was created in Paint. The image is made up of dots or pixels. A photograph is a bitmapped graphic.

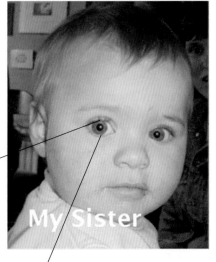

My Sister

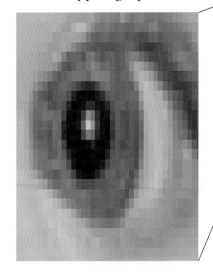

When you stretch a bitmapped graphic the picture becomes fuzzy.

This is a **vector graphic**. It is made up of lots of shapes that are joined to make the image. The shapes can be moved and changed individually. Most clip art images are vector graphics.

A vector graphic can be enlarged without losing any clarity.

Task 2

 Look at **Resource 1.2 Formats**.

1 Stretch Image 1 so that it fills the blue box. It should stay clear.

2 Do the same with Image 2. It should become fuzzy.

3 Image 3 and Image 4 are either a vector graphic or a bitmapped graphic. Which is which?

Task 3

Look at **Resource 1.2 School Information 3** and **Resource 1.2 School Information 4**.

Images have been inserted onto the slides to improve the information. Which do you think works the best?

▶ Skills help

Using scanners and digital cameras with PowerPoint, pages 29–30.

Inserting or placing images into PowerPoint, page 28.

Resource 3.4 Acquiring images

Module Task

a You are going to add your chosen images to your presentation. Decide:
- where do you need to add images to improve the presentation?
- what is the purpose of the image? (look back at Task 1)
- in which format do you need to save the images?

b Create and insert your images by using either a **scanner** or a **digital camera**. If you prefer, you can use clip art, or images from the image bank or the internet. Your teacher will tell you where to access these files.

c Open the presentation created in Unit 1 and insert images where you want them to appear.

d Save your presentation.

Scanner for hand-drawn or printed images.

Digital camera for original photographs.

Copyright

When people do not want others to use images that they have created, they protect them by **copyright**. If anyone else wants to use this image they must get the permission of the person who created it, and sometimes pay a fee. You can see that an image has been copyrighted by the symbol that appears with it. You must take care when you are choosing or using an image that it is not labelled in any way with this copyright symbol.

▶ *Skills help*

Altering clip art images in PowerPoint, pages 28–9.

Task 4

1 *Choose a clipart image which says something about you. Insert it into each slide of your presentation.*

2 *Change the image to suit each slide by enlarging, cropping, rotating or changing the colours.*

3 *Save your presentation.*

Task 5

1 *Print off the slides where you have added images. Are the images the right size and in the right position? Mark any improvements on your printout.*

2 *To work out an effective way to present images and text together you need to find samples of items that you like. Collect a range of items and bring them to the next lesson, including:*
   ● *advertisements*
   ● *news items*
   ● *promotional leaflets*
   ● *logos*
   ● *instruction leaflets or manuals.*

3 *Write a brief description of how the images support the text.*

Unit 1.3
Using fonts and colours

In this unit you will learn how to select and use fonts, font styles and colours to improve the look of your presentation.

Fonts and font attributes

There are many fonts or typefaces to choose from. Some are **modern looking**, some are more traditional. Some are **fun to look at**, others are very easy to read. Some are **Especially Good for Headings** because they stand out.

Serif fonts have little lines on the ends of the letters. Most traditional fonts such as Times New Roman and Bookman are serif fonts. They tend to be used where there is a lot of text on a page such as in a newspaper or novel. This paragraph is set in a serif font.

Sans serif fonts do not have the little lines. They look more modern and are often used in headings. Examples of common sans serif fonts are Arial, Verdana and Helvetica. This paragraph is set in a sans serif font.

Once you have chosen your typeface, you must decide on what other **font attributes** you want to use. You can **format** most fonts in a number of different ways for different purposes:

UPPER CASE
is good for headings, although sometimes

all lower case headings
can be eye catching.

Lower case is usually used if you have a large amount of text because A LOT OF CAPITAL LETTERS TOGETHER CAN BE DIFFICULT TO READ.

Task 1

 Look at **Resource 1.3 Fonts.**

1 How many fonts have been used?

2 How many font sizes have been used?

3 How many font styles are there?

Task 2

 Look at **Resource 1.3 Order.**

1 Use PowerPoint to rearrange the slides into an order that puts the one you like the best as the first slide and so on.

2 Add your reasons for selecting the order of the slides in the **Notes** at the bottom of the slides. For example, you might think that there are too many fonts, they are too big, and the letters are not clear.

3 Print out the **Notes**.

 *Skills help*

Printing in **Note** format in PowerPoint, pages 24–5.

The size of font you choose can make a big **impact** and using **bold**, <u>underline</u> and *italic* can also help to emphasise things. However, you should be careful about using underlining if your copy is going to be viewed on screen because underlining can indicate a hyperlink: www.heinemann.co.uk

Creating the right atmosphere

When creating slides it is important to try and get the right appearance. The way in which fonts are set up can affect how we feel about the text and how easy it is to read.

Colour can add mood: e.g. yellow for danger, red for anger.

Text can be light on dark or dark on light.

Profits are down. We are facing a serious economic crisis.

Font style can be misleading.

Task 3

Look at **Resource 1.3 Font puzzles**.

1 Describe the font you would use for:

- a business letter
- a circus advertisement
- a label on a diagram
- a website address
- a heading on a notice board.

2 Compare your answers with your partners. Did you agree? If not, what was the difference in opinion?

Task 4

Look at **Resource 1.3 Colours**.

1 Look at the way in which the colours have been used on the different slides.

2 Which slide would you use in a presentation about:

- a winter holiday
- a garden centre
- a luxury chocolate bar
- a safari trip.

3 There is still one slide left without a subject. What could that one be used for?

Module Task

a Open the latest version of your presentation.

b Look through the fonts that you have used and check their attributes to see if they match the information on the slide.

c Make changes to fonts or their attributes to improve the presentation.

d Save your presentation.

e Print off the latest version of your presentation and **annotate** it to show where you have made the changes and give reasons why.

 Use different font sizes and styles to help make things stand out rather than changing the colour or font type!

Task 5

1 Before next lesson select five advertisements on the television that make you look at them.

2 Write down the thing that attracts you to the advertisement. Is it colours? Visual effects? Sounds?

3 Which of these advertisements would work if printed in **documents**?

Unit 1.4
Using sounds

In this unit you will learn how to add appropriate sounds to your presentation.

How sound can help

Sounds are very good at making us feel things; they can be used to add atmosphere. Where would the film *Jaws* be without the music?

A sound can be used to give instructions or provide information, especially when there is no presenter, through a **voice-over**. Sound can be set to play continuously or be made to stop and start at the click of a mouse button. It can be designed to happen when an **animation** takes place onscreen, for example when a new heading or subheading appears.

Sound has to be chosen carefully. The purpose of including sound should be obvious. If too many different sounds are added, the audience could become confused as to whether they are meant to watch, read or listen.

Sound sources

Sound files can come from a number of different sources. These include:

- a clip art gallery
- the Internet
- ones created by a **microphone** and recording machine.

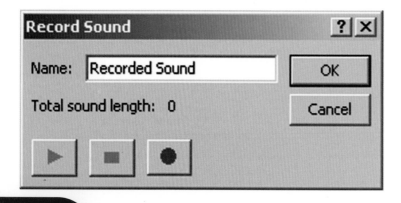

Task 1

Think about the ways in which sound can affect the way we feel.

 *Look at **Resource 1.4 Sounds**, and follow the onscreen instructions. You will also need **Resource 1.4 Sounds like what?** to complete this task.*

1 *Make a list of the sounds that you hear.*

2 *Make up a short story that could use the sounds as sound effects.*

3 *Discuss your story line with a partner.*

▶ *Skills help*

Recording sounds, page 31.

Sound effects are used to make the audience believe that something is happening, for example the sound of raindrops falling to the ground if it is meant to be raining in a radio play. This does not mean that it is actually raining, but that someone has created a sound effect of rain drops.

A *voice-over* is used to provide information about a visual image. A voice-over can add more detail than is given in the text on a screen or it can be a description of an onscreen image.

Recordings can be made to create **sound effects** or a voice-over.

'But where are the horses going to stand to record?'

Task 2

1 Open your presentation, making sure you can add notes for each slide in the **Notes** window.

2 On each slide make notes about the sounds that you **COULD** add to them.

3 Now select very carefully from all the sounds you have listed those that you **SHOULD** add to the presentation.

4 Add in details of how long the sounds should last.

Task 3

1 Open your presentation.

2 Set it up as an automated presentation.

3 Write a script and use a microphone to set up a voice-over that can be set to run as part of your presentation.

4 Practise the timings by viewing each slide before it changes to the next one.

5 Save the latest version of your presentation.

 *Skills help*

Setting up an automated presentation in PowerPoint, page 27.

Module Task

You need to locate the sounds that you decided to use in Task 2. Make sure that you know where to find them.

a *Get the sounds you need by recording them using a microphone and recording machine, find them in the clip art gallery or download them from the Internet.*

b *Open your presentation.*

c *Add in the files and set the correct settings for the duration and running of the sounds.*

d *Run your presentation to make sure that it works as intended.*

e *Save your presentation.*

 Skills help

Inserting sound files into a presentation, pages 30–1.

Task 4

 Look at **Resource 1.4 Sound sense**.

1 *Make an evaluation of your partner's presentation.*

2 *Discuss the evaluation with your partner.*

Task 5

 Use **Resource 1.4 TV Sound log** to help you with this task.

1 *Write down two different time slots when you normally watch television.*

2 *Describe different ways that television presentations are made to attract audiences.*

3 *Bring your notes along to the next lesson.*

Unit 1.5
Changing the style of a presentation

In this unit you will learn how to alter your presentation for different audiences. You will also find out how to set up a presentation so that each slide has the same appearance.

Criteria for a successful presentation

In Unit 1.1 the key **criteria** for creating a successful presentation were identified by thinking about the purpose and the intended audience.

To offer the best possible presentation to an audience there are additional criteria that you will need to think about. These are where, when and how the presentation is to be viewed.

- Will it be viewed in a quiet or noisy place?
- Will it be dark or light in the place?
- Will there be a presenter or will it run automatically?

Task 1

 Look at **Resource 1.5 Performance checklist**.

1 How many of the criteria for successful presentations did you know the answer to before you started work on your presentation?

2 Would the presentation be different if you knew more of the answers?

3 Discuss with a partner how you think your presentation might be affected by each of these criteria.

☆ The look of the slides in a presentation should be altered to suit the audience.

'I think your presentation would suit my dad because he's a big kid!'

Adding backgrounds

Presentation software has a feature that allows you to set a background for the slides. The background can be set to be the same for every slide or different for each slide.

Different backgrounds can suit different audiences. A dark background with white text can be easier to read at a long distance.

Backgrounds can be set:

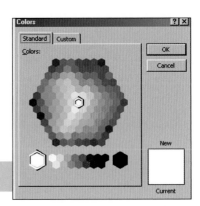

• as a colour

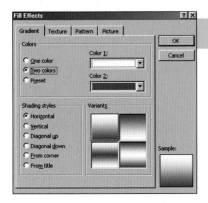

• a gradient fill

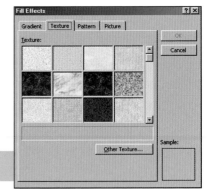

• as a texture

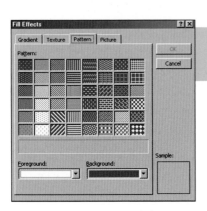

• as a pattern or, if there are some available, as a picture.

Task 2

1 *Browse through the backgrounds that are available.*

2 *Which background would you choose for these different audiences:*
- *children in a playgroup*
- *a swimming club presentation evening*
- *a group of business people?*

 *Skills help*

Working with backgrounds in PowerPoint, pages 25–6.

Presenting to an adult audience

Presentations for an adult audience usually need to look more formal than those aimed at younger people. All the slides should have a similar style. They should not be too fancy or cluttered. Here are some guidelines for making a presentation suitable for an adult audience.

- Use only one background throughout
- Use only a limited range of colours
- Use only two different fonts throughout
- Use the same font style for headings and text throughout
- Use the same layout on each slide
- Use very little sound
- Use very little animation

Module Task

You are to change your presentation to have a consistent appearance and to be suitable for viewing by an audience of teachers and pupils in an assembly hall.

 Use **Resource 1.5 Performance checklist** to help you with this task.

a Create a 'performance checklist' for this new version of your presentation.

b Open your presentation and save it with a different file name to show it is for adults.

c Choose an appropriate background and apply it to all of the slides.

d Make sure that you have used no more than two fonts throughout and that the font style and layout are the same on every slide.

e Check any sounds / animations you have used – are they absolutely necessary for an adult audience? If not, remove them.

f Keep saving your work as you go along. Show the final version of your adult presentation to a partner and watch theirs.

g Use their performance checklist to evaluate their presentation.

Task 3

1 You can set up a **Slide Master** as a background **template** for each slide. A template will place all of the items in the same place on each slide and apply a consistent background and style.

2 Open your presentation.

3 Create a new layout using the **Slide Master**. You will not be able to change this when you are working on the slides, you will have to return to **Slide Master** to edit it.

4 When you are satisfied, check out all slides to see that the layout still works.

▶ Skills help

Working with a storyboard in PowerPoint, page 25.

Working with **Slide Master** in PowerPoint, page 26.

Task 4

1 Print out your slides. Annotate them to show where changes have been made during the lesson, and why. Mark any additional improvements you would like to make.

2 Send a copy of your presentation in **Outline** view to Word to become a storyboard.

3 Use this storyboard to plan changes to the content of your presentation so that it would tell an audience of pupils and teachers about yourself.

In this unit you will learn how to alter the content of the slides in your presentation for a different audience, and how to evaluate a presentation.

Understanding your audience

The content of the slides needs to be suitable for the audience. They should be able to readily understand the content during the presentation. The content can be checked using criteria prompted by the word **PURPOSE**:

P **P**eople in the Audience – Who are they?

U **U**nderstand – Will they understand the words, sounds and images used?

R **R**ead – Will they be able to read the content?

P **P**lanned – Have you planned how to talk about the content?

O **O**ffend – Will any of the content offend the audience?

S **S**imple – Have long, complicated words been used when there are easier ones?

E **E**ffective – Are the text, images and sound clear and effective?

Task 1

 Look at **Resource 1.6 Content checklist** and the storyboard you created in Unit 1.5.

1 Check the content in your revised storyboard presentation.

2 Make notes on the content that needs to be changed to match the **PURPOSE** list.

3 Can you find another way to say things?

4 Can you replace hard words with easier ones?

5 Are all of the images used effectively to help people understand the content?

'So you're telling me that precipitation just means rain?'

Dictionary

Check points

When you have made certain that the content of your presentation matches the criteria for the acronym, PURPOSE, then you need to consider the **layout** of each slide. The layout of the content on the slides should be as clear as possible:

- bullet points should fit on one line
- long sentences or sections of text should be split so they are easy to read
- the slides should not be overcrowded with information
- notes giving additional information can be read or spoken during a presentation
- spelling and grammar should be checked.

Read through all of the content before making a presentation – remember a spellchecker does not know how to spell proper nouns!

Module Task

In Unit 1.5 you planned out a storyboard that showed changes to your presentation to make it suitable for an audience of pupils and teachers.

a Open your presentation.

b Use the storyboard you created to help you to change the presentation to be suitable for the new audience.

c Check the content of each slide against the **PURPOSE** list, and make any further changes necessary.

d Print out your presentation and annotate where the changes have been made.

e Show your presentation to a partner and watch theirs.

Task 2

Look at **Resource 1.6 Transitions** to give you some ideas.

1 Open the latest version of your presentation for the pupil-and-teacher audience.

2 Set it up so that there is a consistent use of slide transitions to make the presentation move between the slides effectively.

3 Experiment with animating different bits of content – but remember the needs of the audience!

Using animation and slide transitions

Presentation software allows you to bring each new piece of content onto the screen, one by one. This is called animation and it can make it easier for the audience to take in what is on the screen.

You can choose different animation styles for different types of content. You can also choose different ways of changing from one slide to the next. This is called **slide transition**.

 Skills help

Working with transitions in PowerPoint, page 26.

Creating animations in PowerPoint, page 27.

Evaluation

You have been evaluating a partner's presentation. To carry out a fair evaluation of a presentation everyone needs to check the same **features**.

The main features to check are:

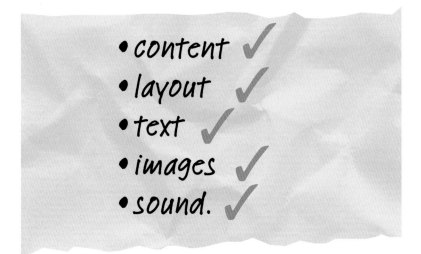

- content ✓
- layout ✓
- text ✓
- images ✓
- sound. ✓

 Look at **Resource 1.6 Evaluation list** to help you with this task.

1 List three different points that you think should be checked for each of the features above. For example, if you are checking the sounds, will it be the volume, the sound itself, or the duration of the sound, and so on?

2 Write this up in the form of an evaluation list.

3 Use your list to evaluate the presentations that you are asked to view.

The Sejour Centre

To complete Module 1 you are to produce a new presentation following the information given below.

Background

The Sejour Centre is an Outdoor Pursuits Centre with the following details:

- close to Paris
- takes 250 visitors at a time
- visitors stay in log cabins.

Activities are:

- canoeing
- climbing
- go-karting
- swimming
- fencing.

Brief

After a visit to the Sejour Centre with your school you have to present the main features and activities of the centre to Year 6 pupils from a local school.

The Year 6 pupils have not been to the centre, but will visit it next year when they are in Year 7. They are all able to read quite well but some of them cannot understand long words.

Your presentation should not have more than six slides in it and will be seen by the pupils during an assembly in the school hall.

Use your knowledge from all of the units in Module 1 to help you to create a presentation for these pupils. When you have finished your presentation, make notes on how you would change it to make it more suitable for an audience which included Year 6 pupils' parents as well. Create a second version of your presentation, taking in these changes.

Plan carefully!

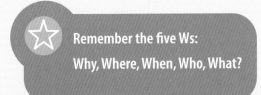

Remember the five Ws:
Why, Where, When, Who, What?

The following notes all refer to PowerPoint for Office 2000. If you are using a different version, some of the screens may look slightly different, but they should contain similar options.

Software skills

Saving a presentation

1 On the **Menu** bar click on **File, Save**.

2 Type a name for your presentation.

3 Click on **Save** or press **Enter**.
4 To save an existing file with a new file name, click on **File, Save As** and then repeat steps 2–3.

Switching views

1 Click on the **Slide View** or **Outline View** icons at the bottom left of the screen.

Changing slide order

1 Click on **View, Slide Sorter**.

2 Holding down the mouse button, click and drag the slide to the correct place.

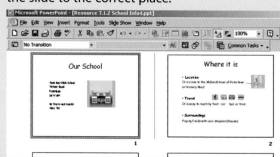

3 Click on **View, Slide** to return to slide **View**.

Adding, viewing and printing speaker notes

1 Go to the slide where you want to add speaker notes.
2 Click on **View, Notes Page**.

3 Type your notes.

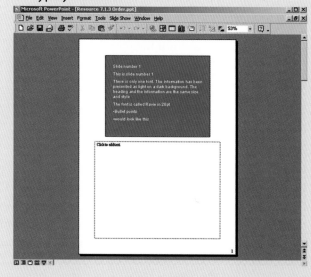

4 Click on **Close**.

To view your notes
5 Click on **View**, **Notes Page**.

To print your notes
6 Click on **File**, **Print**.

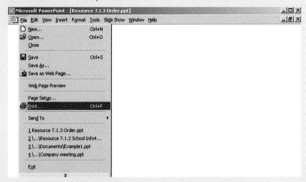

7 Under **Print What**, select **Notes Pages**.

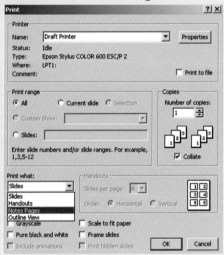

8 Click on **OK**.

Creating storyboards
1 Click on **File**, **Send To**, **Microsoft Word**.

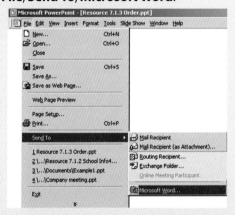

2 Select a layout.
3 Click on **OK**.

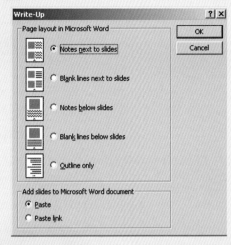

Using backgrounds
1 Click on **Format**, **Background**.

Changing background colours
2 Click on the down arrow.
3 Click on **More Colours**.

4 Select a colour.
5 Click on **OK**.

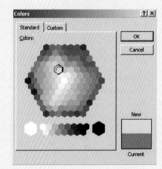

Using fill effects

6 Click on **Fill effects**.

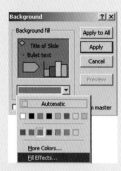

7 Click on **Texture** or **Pattern** Tab and select one.

8 Click on **OK**.

9 Click on **Apply** to change one slide or **Apply To All** to change all slides.

Using slide master

1 Click on **View**, **Master**, **Slide Master**.

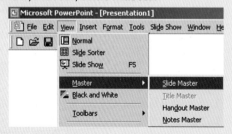

2 Click on each of the elements and change font size, typeface, style and colour as you wish.

3 Insert date and time, footer text and slide number in the boxes at the bottom if you wish.

4 Add a background if you wish.

5 To add a new slide master click on the **New Slide Master** button on the **Slide Master View** toolbar.

6 To add a new title master click on the **Insert, New Title Master** button on the main toolbar, or click on **Insert, New Title Master**.

7 When you are happy click on **Close** on the master tool bar.

Transition from one slide to another

1 Click on **Slide Show**, **Slide Transition**

2 Click on the down arrow in the **Effect** window to choose how you want the transition to happen. Choose the speed: Fast, Medium or Slow.

3 In the **Advance** pane, choose whether to advance on mouse click or automatically. If you choose automatically, use the up and down arrows to choose how long before you move to the next slide.

4 Click the down arrow in the **Sound** window to choose any sound you want to accompany the transition.

5 Click **Apply** to change one slide, or **Apply to All** to change all slides.

Using animations

1 Click on the picture, graph or text box you want to animate.
2 Click on **Slide Show**, **Custom Animation**.

3 On the **Effects** tab, click on the down arrow under **Entry animation and sound**.

4 Choose an animation action.
5 Click on **OK**.

During your slide show, the animation for the selected object will run when you click the mouse. If you want the animation to run automatically, then do the following:

6 Click on the **Order & Timing** tab.

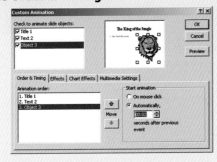

7 Click on the **Automatically** button in the Start animation pane.
8 Click on **OK**.
9 Click on the **Preview** button to view the animation.

Running your slide show automatically

1 Click on **Slide Show**, **Rehearse Timings**.

2 A timer window appears.

3 After each slide has played, press the spacebar on the keyboard. When all of the slides have played, click on **Yes** to save the timings.

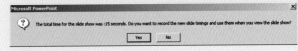

Text skills

Adding

1 Click on **Insert**, **Text Box**.

2 Holding down the mouse button, click and drag to create a text box.

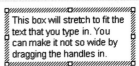

3 Type your information. The box will automatically stretch to fit the text.

Changing text

You can change the colour, font, size and style.
1 Highlight the text that you want to change.
2 Click on **Format**, **Font**.

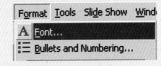

To change the font
3 Scroll down the **Font** window and click on the font that you want to use.

To change the font style
4 Click on the style that you want.

To change font size
5 Scroll down the **Size** window and click on the size you want.

To change the colour

6 Click on the down arrow under **Colour**.

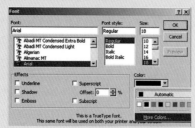

7 Select **More Colours** and choose the colour for your text.

8 When you are happy with everything, click on **OK** twice.

Image skills

Inserting images

1 Click on **Insert**, **Picture**.

To insert a piece of clip art

2 Click on **Clip Art**.

3 Click on the **Pictures** tab.

4 Select a category.

5 Select the clip art or picture you would like to use.

6 Click on the **Insert Clip** icon.

To insert a picture from the Internet using Internet Explorer

7 Minimise PowerPoint.

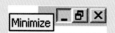

8 Go to the web page where the picture you want to import is located.

9 Right-click on the picture.

10 Left-click on **Copy**.

11 Minimise Internet Explorer and maximise PowerPoint.

12 Click on **Edit**, **Paste**.

Altering clip art images in Powerpoint

1 Click on the image. The picture toolbar appears.

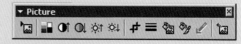

To crop the image

2 Click on the **Crop** button.

3 Put the pointer over any of the handles on the image – turns into a crop button.

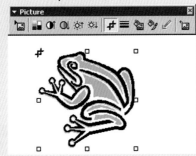

4 Click and drag the handles to crop the image.
5 When you have finished cropping, click on the crop button again to return to the normal pointer.

To add a border
6 Click on the **Line Style** button and choose the style of line you require.

To recolour the picture
7 Click on the **Recolour Picture** button. The **Recolour Picture** dialogue box appears.

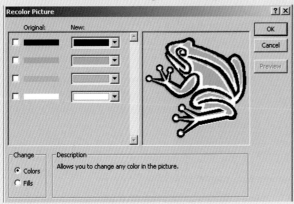

8 If you want to leave one of the colours the same, click the box in the **Original** column.
9 If you want to change one of the colours click the down arrow on that colour in the **New** column.
10 Click on **More colours**. Select the colour you want.
11 Click on **OK**.
12 When you have made all the changes you want, click on **OK**.

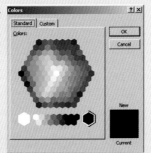

To reset the picture
13 At any time you can click on the **Reset picture** button to return the image to its original state.

Using a scanner

1 Go to the slide where you want to insert the picture.
2 Put the picture into the scanner.
3 Click on **Insert**, **Picture**, **From Scanner or Camera**.

4 Click on the down arrow to select your scanner software.
5 Click on **Insert**.

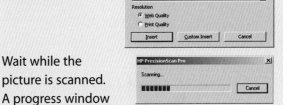

6 Wait while the picture is scanned. A progress window will show.
7 Click and drag the mouse to select the portion of the image you want to scan.
8 When scanning is complete, the picture you have scanned will appear on your Powerpoint slide.

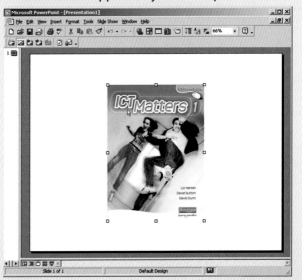

Using a digital camera

To use a digital camera for an image you will need to ask how yours is set up. You will be able to take photographs as with any camera. The difference is that the camera stores images in a digital format. The photograph can then be downloaded onto a computer.

You can download photographs from a floppy disc, memory stick or through a data connection cable.

You can look at the images before you download them and save or delete them.

You can replace deleted ones by taking new ones.

Creating vector graphics

Make sure you can see the **Drawing** toolbar.

To make the Drawing toolbar appear
1 Click on **View, Toolbars**.
2 Select **Drawing**.

To create your own graphic
3 Select a shape, by either clicking on **AutoShapes** and choosing one, or by clicking on one of the shapes on the toolbar.
4 Click and drag your mouse to create the shape in the size that you want.
5 Click on the **Fill Colour, Line Colour** and **Line Style** icons on the Drawing toolbar and select the colours and styles you want for your graphic.
6 When you are happy with it, click anywhere else on the screen.

You can group several shapes to make them into one shape.

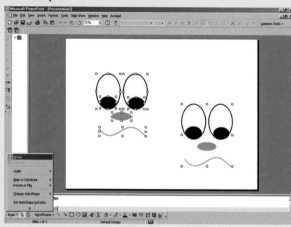

7 Hold down the shift key and click on all the shapes you want to group.
8 Click on **Draw, Group** (you may need to expand the dialogue box to see this option).
9 Click anywhere else on the screen.

Sound skills

Inserting sounds

Sound files can be inserted from the Gallery or from the Internet.

To insert a sound from the Gallery
1 Click on **Insert, Movies and Sounds, Sound from Gallery**.
2 Select a sound in the same way as you select a clip art image. A speaker icon will appear on your slide.

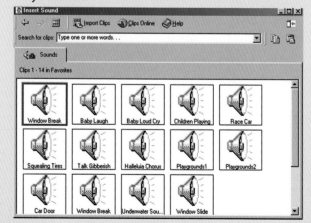

To insert a sound from the Internet

3 Follow the same procedure as you did to insert an image from the Internet. You can add your sounds to the Gallery.

Recording sounds

1 Plug in a microphone to your computer.

2 Click on **Insert**, **Movies and Sounds**, **Record Sound**.

3 Click on the **Record** button and talk or play the sound you want to record.

4 Click on the **Stop** button when you have finished recording.

5 Click on the **Play** button to hear what you have recorded.

6 To change what you have recorded, click on the **Cancel** button and repeat from Step 1.

7 When you are happy with your recording, click on **OK**. A sound speaker icon will appear on your slide.

Playing sounds in your presentation

To play sounds manually, click on the sound speaker icon in your slideshow. You must be in Slideshow mode to hear the sounds.

To play sounds automatically

1 Click on the sound speaker icon you want to play automatically.

2 Click on **Slide Show**, **Custom Animation**.

3 Click on the **Order & Timing** tab.

4 Click on the **Automatically** button on the Start animation pane.

5 Click on the up arrow or the down arrow to choose the number of seconds between the animation actions.

6 Click on **OK**.

Hiding a speaker icon

1 Click on the sound speaker icon you want to hide.

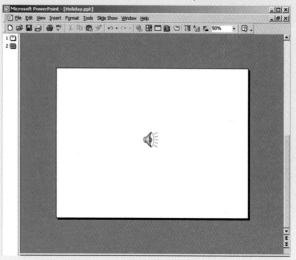

2 Drag the sound speaker icon to a grey area.

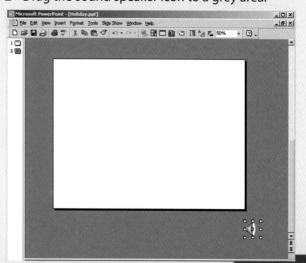

In this module you will be learning how to find out if data is **fit for its purpose**. You will use the **Internet** to find information and evaluate websites.

Before you start there are some skills and words that you will need to know. Read about each skill in the boxes below and then decide which of the following statements best describes how you feel about it:

A I am confident that I understand / can do this.
B I think I understand / can do this, but I would like to check.
C I definitely don't know how to do this and I need to learn.

Searching electronic sources

In a book the only way to find information quickly is to look in the contents list or the index. Electronic sources have other quicker ways of locating information. Many do have an **index**, but they also often have a **search** facility and / or a **browse** facility.

Index. This is an alphabetical list of **key words**.

Key word. This is a word which can be used in a search.

Search. Many CD-ROMs and websites have a search option. You type in a key word and the computer will find all the appearances of the word you are looking for.

Browse. Many electronic sources provide a list of all the types of information they contain. You can scroll down until you find what you are looking for.

Using the Internet

The *Internet* is an enormous network of computers. They are not actually linked together except through connections to the **World Wide Web (www)**.

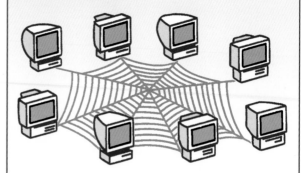

World Wide Web (www). This is the name that is given to a collection of information held on the Internet. The www is made up of **websites**.

Website. A website is made up of a set of **web pages** that are about the same subject. There are various types of websites, including those used to display information, those which sell products and those which are just for fun.

Web pages. These are like pages in a book. They are linked together in a website. Each web page may have different topics on it but normally will have the same theme, for example they might all be about Egypt.

Home Page. This is the first screen that is displayed when you open a website.

Conducting a survey

A way of finding out what a range of people think about something. A **survey** is carried out using a **questionnaire**. Surveys can take place in the street, online, by telephone, through magazines and newspapers.

Questionnaire. This is a series of questions that are written specially to find out what people think about something.

The words below and their meanings have been jumbled up. Can you match each word to its correct meaning?

Survey	A worldwide network of computers
www	A list of questions
URL	A way of finding out what people think
Web browser	The unique address of a website
Web pages	A collection of information held on the Internet
Website	Uniform Resource Locator
Website address	Software we use to access the www
Questionnaire	The individual screens of a website

Unit 2.1
Information for a purpose

What is an information source?

An **information source** is the place you find information you need for a particular purpose. Sometimes, it can be difficult to know how to **locate** the information you need because there are so many possible sources: books, newspapers, letters, radio, television, magazines, leaflets, brochures, the Internet, CD ROMs, pictures, people… the list could go on for ever.

Most information is in the form of text, but information can be something that you sense. For instance, if you are about to cross the street and you hear a car horn – what does that tell you?

What is the information for?

In order to know where to look for information, you need to be clear about the purpose for which it will be used. For example, if I asked you to find me some information about the weather in Peru, you would probably give me different information depending on which of these purposes I said I had:

- I am researching weather patterns in South America over the last century
- I am planning a sightseeing holiday.

Task 1

1 Write down five sources of information that are around you at the moment.

2 Write down the type of information that they provide.

3 Do you believe the information you receive from all of these sources?

Task 2

1 Write down the differences you think there might be between the information required by a weather researcher and a holiday maker.

2 Suggest some suitable sources for each person's information.

Surveys and questionnaires

These people are gathering information in an opinion poll.

Sometimes it is useful to gather information from a large number of sources. This is called doing a **survey**. Governments sometimes want to find out the **viewpoint** of voters on a particular issue, such as 'Should Britain join the Euro?' They may commission an **opinion poll** in which people are asked to vote Yes or No on that issue. This is a kind of survey.

Companies often use surveys to find out what their customers want. They ask their customers to complete a **questionnaire**. This is a list of questions on a particular topic. The answers are collected together into a report, which then becomes an information source which the company will use to help them decide what products to make and sell.

 *Skills help*

Writing questions for questionnaires, page 47.

Making a questionnaire

The way you word a question can affect the response you get. You need to be sure what you are trying to find out before you write the questions. The table below lists some of the main types of questions used in questionnaires.

Task 3

 Look at **Resource 2.1 Questions** before you start this task.

Suggest which type of question might be best for the following purposes:

1 To find out which are the most popular rides at a theme park.

2 To get ideas for new rides.

3 To find out if there is anything that people really dislike about a theme park.

4 To find out if people recognise the brand name of the theme park.

Question type	Example	Response
Open-ended opinion	Which do you like?	Wide range of answers – useful if you want to find out new information
Closed questions	Do you like fruit?	Yes/No
Multiple choice	Is the answer A, B, C or D	Only one right answer
Ordered	Put the following in the order that you like best	Popularity of responses
Selected – viewpoint	Select your three favourites from this list	Popularity of responses

It is important to know the reason for asking a question before you can work out how to word the question.

The response you get can also be affected by who you ask, and how many people you ask. Again you need to choose these carefully depending on your purpose.

'How long is a piece of string?'

Selecting a sample

Each person has his or her own opinions which might be the same as a lot of other people's opinions or they might be completely unique. The only way to find out is to ask a lot of people the same questions and compare the answers they all give. The people who are chosen to answer the questions are called a **sample**. If enough people in the sample give a similar answer to a question then it can be assumed that this is a generally held opinion and not just an individual viewpoint.

Market research companies and opinion pollsters take great care selecting the people to answer their questionnaires. They need to be sure that the sample is **representative** of the total number of people who could have answered the questionnaire. In order to do this they first draw up a profile of the type of person they want to ask.

Task 4

 Look at **Resource 2.1 Cats** to help you start thinking about survey samples.

You have been asked to do a survey to find out what people think is a good snack.

1. Write down three things that you might need to know before you start asking any questions.

2. Ask three people in your class the question 'What is a good snack?' Write down the answers you get.

3. Write down two things that you definitely know from the answers you have been given, without asking anyone else any more questions.

4. What things do you not know?

Case study – choosing a representative sample

A UK chain of burger bars wants to know what teenagers think of a new type of hamburger before they introduce it in their shops. What type of person should they ask?

Teenagers *– only those people between the ages of 13 and 19.*

In the UK *– because that is where their shops are.*

People who eat burgers *– they may use existing customers.*

Once they have decided on the type of person they want to question, they can select a sample of, say, 1000 people who match the criteria above. They would probably make sure that they had an equal number of boys and girls in each age group 13–19, and that they had a good geographical spread across the country, in order to make it a fair sample.

Module Task

A company 'UWish' wants to find out about teenagers and activity holidays in order to help them plan what they will offer next year.

 Look at **Resource 2.1 Holidays** and **Resource 2.1 Survey**.

a Summarise in your own words what you think the company wishes to find out.

b You are going to produce a questionnaire to help them find the answers. Write down six questions that should go on the questionnaire. Remember to think about the different types of questions you can use.

c You are going to test out the questionnaire on some people in your school. Decide who you want to answer the questionnaire. Things to think about are: Are they boys or girls? How old are they? Should they all be from the same class?

d Print out a copy of your questions and ask the students you have chosen for their responses.

e What conclusions can you draw from the responses you get? Record any information that you could feed back to 'UWish'. You may find it helpful to show your findings in a chart.

f How accurate do you think this information is?

Before the next lesson you are to plan a location map for visitors to find your school.

1 What information do you need to be able to create the map?

2 Write a list of the information points you would have to know.

▶ Skills help

Understanding charts, page 47.

Selecting sources and finding information

How to locate information

Knowing the type of information that you need should help you to locate it. For instance, if you wanted to know the time of the next bus to a local town, there would be a number of sources you could use:

- bus timetable
- website
- telephone
- people.

Selecting the right one of these would depend on where you were.

- A bus timetable is only useful if you have one!
- A website is only useful if you have access to the Internet.
- A telephone is only useful if you have one and know the bus company's name.
- People are useful most of the time, provided they know the information.

Any one of these would give you the information, but you would have to decide which was the most efficient way at the time you needed information.

Finding, or sourcing, information is only successful if you know exactly what you want. For example, finding information about the Tudors may sound easy. They were the English kings and queens who reigned from 1485–1603. But what about the people called Tudor who are living now? Does it include them?

Task 1

What is the most efficient way to:

1. *Get up-to-date information that changes every hour?*

2. *Find out if the information you need is in a book?*

3. *Get telephone contact details for all local CD and video shops?*

Finding information on the Internet

One major source of information is the **Internet**. A **web browser** is used to access the Internet. This opens the **World Wide Web (www)**, which contains a great many **websites**, each containing a number of pages. It is a bit like a library containing many books. A website can be thought of as one source, in the same way as a book is one source.

Websites might look very different, but most of them work in the same way.

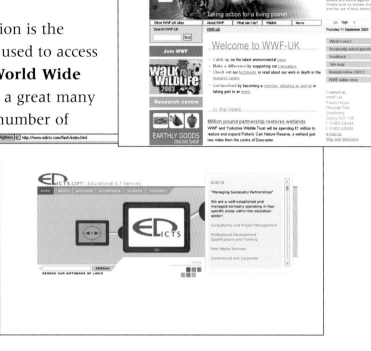

Searching for information within a website

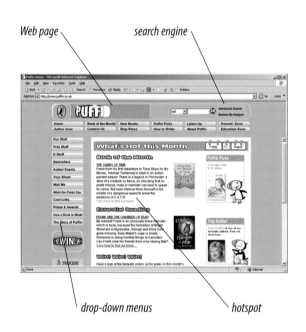

Web page

search engine

drop-down menus

hotspot

Information on websites tends to be organised in a similar way to that in books – it is grouped into topic areas, or chapters, and there is usually an **index** or **key word search** facility as well. (There is more information about using search and **browse** facilities in the Prior learning section on page 32.)

Some websites have additional features to make it even easier to find the information you need. For example they may use **drop-down menus**, which allow you to quickly see the different types of information available, or **hotspots**, which take you instantly to a different part of the website. Many websites have a **site map**, which gives you an overview of the whole site (a bit like a **contents page** in a book).

Task 2

 Look at **Resource 2.2 Web page**.

Mark on the web page where you would go to:
- find out if some information is on the website
- use a drop-down menu
- use a hotspot
- use a search engine
- go back to previous web page.

☆ As web pages take time to appear, each click to a new web page will take more time. It is important to navigate around websites efficiently.
Planning what information you need before you get to a website will help you to search efficiently.

 Skills help

The Internet; more key terms, page 49.

Looking for a suitable website on the Internet

Sometimes you do not know which websites contain good information. You may have been told to research a particular topic, such as the Tudors. How would you find some suitable websites to look on? Luckily there are a number of very powerful **search engines**, which can help you to locate the information you need on the Internet. You have probably heard of some of these.

You can access these search engine websites by typing their **URL (Uniform Resource Locator)** or **web address** into your web browser. When the search screen comes up, you can type in the topic you want to find out about and start the search. The search engine will search the entire World Wide Web and come up with a list of links to websites which match the **search criteria** (or topics) that you put in. Some websites such as Yahooligans.com will come up with fewer results than others because they only select websites suitable for children.

Refining a search

The text entered in a search should be as precise as possible. If you simply enter the word **London** into Google.com you will get literally millions of links – 32 million!

Now try typing in **London** and **England**. You will immediately reduce the number of results to just over 3 million. Further details can be added to the search. For example, entering **London** and **England** and **Palaces** gets you down to 43,700, and if you then type in **London** and **England** and **Palaces** and **Tudors** you get down to 498.

This process of adding detail is called **refining** your search.

Task 3

1 Use a search engine to find information about blue whales for a conservation project.

2 How many results did you get?

3 Use a different search engine and type in the same search.

4 How many results did you get?

5 Which site gives most relevant information – quickly?

6 Can you improve your search technique?

7 Try different searches to see if you can limit your results.

☆ The more precise you are in stating what you want to find, the better your chances of getting good information back.

Module Task

 Look at **Resource 2.2 Sharks!** to help you with this task.

An aquarium is well known for its conservation work and has just started a programme to allow people to go scuba-diving with sharks.

a Access the website by going to http://www.heinemann.co.uk/hotlinks.

b Keep a record of the number of web pages that you need to visit in order to find out:
- where the aquarium is
- the opening times
- the cost of diving with the sharks as an unqualified diver
- any restrictions that there are on diving
- any special events happening this month.

c Was the website easy to navigate? Could you find the information easily? Was it easy to read the web pages?

Task 4

The website offers the chance to take part in an online Deep Sea Adventure.

Find out from the Captain's Log:

1 What are the Northern Delights?

2 Name three types of shark behaviour that you might see.

Task 5

You are planning the perfect day out with a friend.

1 List ten criteria that you would need to meet to make the day a success.

2 Write a list of the information points you would have to know.

'Perfect!'

Are things always what they seem?

As we have discovered, information comes from many different sources.

There may be more than one possible source of the same information. It is important to choose the source which provides the most **reliable** information for your purpose.

Should we believe all that we read, hear, see or are told? Just because something looks and sounds official doesn't mean it necessarily is. Knowing the source can make us feel more confident about the information. However, even official or trusted sources may only reveal part of the story. You may need to go to more than one source to get the whole picture.

If text and images are in electronic format, then it is very easy to copy, edit and change them using ICT. This makes the job of deciding which information is reliable more difficult. Often it is helpful to compare more than one source.

Task 1

 *Look at **Resource 2.3 What it says**. Read the articles carefully.*

1 *Would you have believed these articles?*

2 *Is there a clue, or sign, that makes you trust the information?*

3 *Can you think of other ways to check that the information can be believed?*

Task 2

 Look at **Resource 2.3 Words**.

This description of an autumn night in London needs to change to match the picture.

1 Use your word processing skills to make your own version. One change has been done for you (you might want to change it!)

2 Change any words you want to make the description match the picture.

3 Save your work.

4 Print a copy and compare your new description with a partner's.

Where does the information come from?

In Unit 2.2 you learnt about searching for websites containing information on a particular topic. You narrowed your search down to a few hundred, but how do you then decide which one(s) of those to use? One way is to look at the name of the website. That can give you some clues about how reliable it might be.

Domain names

The bit of a web address after the last full stop is called the **domain name**. A domain name is a guide to the type of website that it is. You can look at the domain name in a website address before opening the website. This can save visiting websites that are not going to be the type you want. Many websites end with '.com'. This tells you that the website belongs to a **COM**pany, so it will be a commercial organisation aiming to make money from the information on its website. Here are some other commonly used domain names:

.org   .gov   .co.uk   .ac

What type of websites might these be?

'I used to know someone called Dot Com.'

 Skills help

Understanding domain names, page 49.

Module Task

 *Look at **Resource 2.3 Comparisons**.*

To carry out this task you will compare official and unofficial websites for information about Disney.

The websites can be accessed by going to http://www.heinemann.co.uk/hotlinks.

a *View the websites, then find information on each of the following:*
- *what you can do when you are at Walt Disney World*
- *a plan of a five-day visit to Walt Disney World*
- *the person, Walt Disney*
- *how to get to Disneyland*
- *where to book cheapest holidays*
- *where and how to play an online game.*

b *Which website would you recommend as the best at providing information on each item?*

Task 3

The personal feelings of authors can affect the way information is presented in websites.

Look at the two websites about Christopher Columbus, which can be found at http://www.heinemann.co.uk/hotlinks.

1 *Which of the websites :*
- *provides a range of viewpoints about his travels?*
- *gives most information about his life?*

2 *Can you tell where the website authors got their information from?*

3 *Can you locate any better sites?*

Stratford from the Internet

To complete Module 2 you are to produce a guide for visitors on finding information relevant to their needs from the Internet.

Background

Some overseas visitors are spending their holiday in this country. They want to get information about places to visit connected with Shakespeare and his life.

Brief

You are to produce an Internet Guide that will be given out to overseas visitors when they visit travel agents to find out about Stratford-upon-Avon and the surrounding area.

Use a search engine to help you to compile a list of websites for the visitors to look at before their visit. You should aim to have at least five sites on your list.

 The **Module 2 Assignment worksheet** can be used to make your list.

In order to decide which are the best websites you should think about:
- What are the types of thing that a visitor would want to do?
- What do they need to know?
- Where might they stay?
- How relevant will the information be to people from abroad?

For each of the websites on your list, write a short paragraph for the visitors, stating:
- why they should look at the site
- what the points of interest on it are
- how easy it is to use
- whether you think it is an 'official' or an 'unofficial' website.

Save your work with a suitable file name.

 Present the list as a ratings chart to show the best sites for people to visit:

Brilliant ✪ ✪ ✪ ✪ ✪
Poor ✪

Writing questions for questionnaires

There are different types of questions that you can use on a questionnaire to make people respond as you want them to.

Open questions
(e.g. What type of sports do you like?)

Answers will be people's opinions. There could be a wide variety of answers and all could be correct. The conclusions would have to be put together in a report or mark scheme that identified all of the different responses.

Closed questions
People are given a small number of possible answers to choose from, so the results can be counted or quantified. Conclusions from closed questions can be presented as a score, such as 8 out of 10, or as a percentage of the total, for example 80%. Sometimes they are presented on a graph or chart.

There are various different types of closed question:

Yes or No
(e.g. Do you like soccer?)
You can add up the number of people who said yes and the number who said no.

Multiple choice
(e.g. Is a mug A, B, C, D?)
There is only one right answer. The total of the right answers gives a score. This kind of question is used to find out how much people know about something. It is sometimes used in school exam papers!

Ordered list
(e.g. Put in order the fastest cars.)
This helps to find out what people like best. It provides a comparison between the items on the list. Results could be drawn as a graph or chart.

Selected list
(e.g. Pick three of these from the list.)
The same as an Ordered list.

Charts

The most common form of charts used to show conclusions from surveys are bar charts and pie charts.

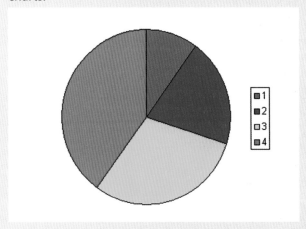

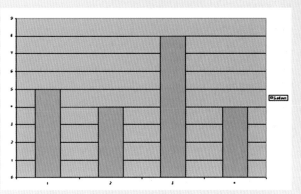

More information about creating charts can be found in the Skills help sections of Modules 4 and 5.

Using tables in MS Word

What is a table?

A table is set up in rows and columns.

Each individual rectangle in the table is called a cell.

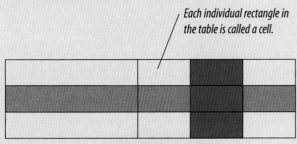

This table has three rows and four columns.

You can change the way that text appears in a cell by using the normal format toolbar.

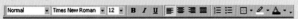

You can enter text into each of the cells in a table by clicking on the cell.

You can move between cells using the Arrow keys on your keyboard.

Deleting rows and columns

1   Click in the row or column that you want to delete.
2   Click **Table**, **Delete**, **Rows** OR **Table**, **Delete**, **Columns**.

Inserting a row

1   Click in a row that is above or below where you want the new one to be.
2   Click on **Table**, **Insert**, **Rows Above** OR **Table**, **Insert**, **Rows Below**.

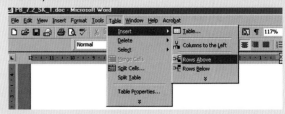

Inserting columns

1   Click on the table in a column to the left or right of where you want the new column.
2   Click **Table**, **Insert**, **Columns to the Left** OR **Table**, **Insert**, **Columns to the Right**.

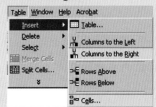

Changing text colour

1   Highlight the text whose colour you want to change (it could be a letter, a word, a paragraph or a whole document).
2   Click on the **font colour** icon from the **Format** toolbar and choose the colour you want.

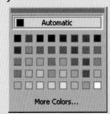

The Internet

Web browser. This is a software program that is used to access the Internet. It opens the World Wide Web – www.

Navigation toolbar. This is a toolbar that appears above a screen display, that allows a user to Save, Print, Search and move between pages or websites.

Uniform Resource Locator (URL). Every website has a URL. This is the website address that no other website has. It is unique like a house address. URLs are used to identify where the files that make up a website are stored.

Website address. Website addresses are normally written in the same way. Most begin with http://www followed by the name of the website. For example, http://www.disney.go.com is a Disney Website.

Search engine. A website which allows you to search the whole World Wide Web and bring back a list of websites which relate to the subject you are interested in. Examples of search engines are Google, Yahoo, Alta Vista, BBCi.

Domain names. A website address is split up into sections. For example:
http://www.bbc.co.uk
is split up as:
http://www. locates the website on the www
bbc. is the company or organisation that owns the website
co.uk is the domain name. '.uk' means that it comes from the UK. If it was '.au' it would be located in Australia.
There are some common domain names used:

.org	is used by ORGanisations

.gov	is used by GOVernment agencies

.com	is used by commercial COMpanies

.co.uk	is also used by commercial companies, but ones located in the UK who want people to know their country

.net	is used by companies for InterNET activities.

Module 3
Making a leaflet

In this module you will learn how to use a **desktop publishing (DTP)** program to design and produce the front cover for a newsletter about your school, and then how to transfer the text and images to form a leaflet.

Before you start there are some skills and words that you will need to know. Some of them are the same as the skills you needed for Module 1, so you can look them up there if you need to remind yourself. Read about each skill in the boxes below and then decide which of the following statements best describes how you feel about it:

A I am confident that I understand / can do this.
B I think I understand / can do this, but I would like to check.
C I definitely don't know how to do this and I need to learn.

> **Log on to the school network**
> (see Module 1)

> **Use a shared area to load and save work** (see Module 1)

> **Move text and pictures** (see Module 1)

> **Use the file names suggested by the school** (see Module 1)

> **Copy and paste text and pictures** (see Module 1)

> **Use desktop publishing (DTP) software**
>
> Desktop publishing software allows you to place, move, **rotate**, **crop** and change text and images. It is much more flexible than word processing software, but many of the tasks you can carry out are the same, for example editing, inserting, deleting, moving, copying and pasting. Newspapers, magazines and some books are created using desktop publishing software.
>
> *Rotate.* This means to turn an image or text around.
>
> *Crop.* This means to remove part of an image using a software tool. It is like using a pair of scissors to cut a bit of a picture. The difference is, if you change your mind you can change the cropping to show the image again.

Enter text into a DTP document

In desktop publishing software you add text into a document with a **text frame**.

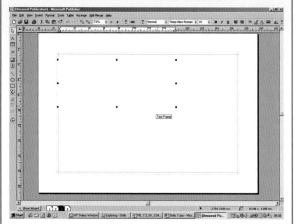

Text frame. This is a box that you set up on the screen. You can add text into the frame. The frame can be moved or placed in front of or sent behind other frames. This is called **layering**.

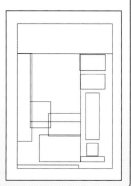

Insert pictures into a DTP document

You can get images through clip art, from other saved files, or via a camera or a scanner. If you get the images directly from a digital camera or scanner it is called **acquiring** the images.

Acquiring. When an image is needed, software looks for a connection to a scanner or a camera. If there are connections then you can choose which way you want to get a picture into your document. If you make a mistake you can cut the image out of the document.

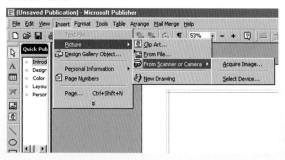

Cut. If you cut an image you remove it from the document completely.

Task

1 Log on to the school network and go to the shared area. Find and open the file called **Resource 3 Circus poster**. Save a version of it to your part of the shared area. Give it an appropriate file name.

2 Create a text frame in the bottom right-hand corner of the poster. Enter the following text into the frame: **Special attraction – Mico and his Marvellous Mice. One week only!** Change the font to make it stand out.

3 **Import** the image Mouse.bmp. Make any changes you want to the image. When you are happy with it, move it to the space at the bottom right of the poster near the text you have entered.

4 Save your final version under a new file name (for example put v1 at the end).

In this unit you will learn about how design can be used to create a corporate image. You will begin to plan your newsletter.

What is a corporate image?

A **corporate image** is created when an organisation, such as a company, group, or even a school, decides to produce an overall 'look' for all of their materials. This look will give an impression of the organisation. The main materials that organisations use to produce their corporate images are:

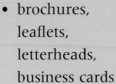

- clothing, uniforms

- brochures, leaflets, letterheads, business cards

- websites

How is it created?

An organisation discusses a **design brief** with a designer or group of designers. The design brief gives the designers a framework to follow and base their ideas on. It helps them to get the right feel in the layout and style for the image. It has some common features that are easily recognisable, appeal to the right **audience** and reflect the organisation.

Corporate images are built by the use of features such as **logos**, text styles, colour schemes, and shapes.

- What shape is a Coca-Cola bottle?
- What colour is a Kit-Kat?

- products, manufactured goods

Look at **Resource 3.1 Corporate**.

It shows web pages from a famous company.

1 Write down a list of items that are used to build the corporate image on these web pages.

2 Write down how the web pages are different.

3 Why do you think they are different?

4 Why do companies want a corporate image?

To set up a corporate image for printed materials you need to consider which features are going to be used to create the image. For example: will the logo always appear in a certain place? Is there a theme colour or a special **font** to use?

ICT makes it very easy to create **templates** so that the features which form a corporate image can be repeated in a series of related documents. Different elements such as text and images can be layered one on top of the other.

 A corporate image can be good or bad for an organisation. If an organisation is successful then people link their image with success, if they fail, then the image is recognised as a failure!

'I think the uniform of Parrot Street Junior is a bit off!'

Task 2

 Look at **Resource 3.1 Adverts**.

1 Make notes about the way the corporate image has been developed in the adverts.

2 List four things that do not change from one advert to the next and four items that do change.

3 What type of audience do you think the company is interested in?

Task 3

 Look at **Resource 3.1 Names**.

1 What type of organisation does the name make you think about?

2 Who are they trying to appeal to?

3 Think of a trendy name for a new company that is setting up a web-based service. Explain how you could create a corporate image around the name.

Newsletters

In this module you are creating the front cover for a newsletter about your school. Many organisations use regular newsletters to keep their members or customers informed about their activities. Here are some examples:

Produced by	For
Clubs	football fans, youth groups
Businesses	clients and shareholders, other businesses
Communities	local level, national level
Organisations	political parties, hobby enthusiasts
Manufacturers	customers, suppliers

 *Skills help*

Adding pages to a Publisher document, page 74–5.

Task 4

 Look at **Resource 3.1 Layers**.

1 Identify how the text, background colour and images have been arranged as **layered objects**.

2 Select all of the elements and copy them.

3 Add a new page to the document. Paste all the elements into the new page. You are going to make this page into the front page of the next issue, so start by altering the date. Will you also change the date font or not?

4 Decide which elements should change and which should remain the same. Change those which need changing.

5 Save your work.

Module Task

You are going to plan the front cover for your school newsletter. This is the design brief: it must be one side of A4 and it must contain the title of the newsletter, the school logo, the issue date, some images and some text. It is up to you to decide:

- whether it will be **portrait** or **landscape**
- how many text boxes there should be and where they should go
- how many images to use
- how large the title and headings will be
- what colours and fonts to use.

In this unit you will work on the basic design for the cover, thinking especially about which elements make up the school's corporate image.

 Look at **Resource 3.1 Newsletter** to give you some ideas.

a Either save a version of **Resource 3.1 Newsletter**, or create a new document in your DTP package. Save it as 'My Newsletter'. If you do not have a DTP package, you can use Word.

b Create text boxes for your newsletter cover and label them, setting font size and style. For example, in the date box, type 'Date' in the font size and style you want the date to be.

c Print out your work and save it in the **shared area**.

 Skills help

Creating text boxes (frames), in Publisher, page 75.

Setting up a document in Publisher, page 73–5.

Pointers for a good design

Although designers follow a design brief it usually leaves them room for creative decisions about layout and the general feel of a design. For example, a design brief will inform them that:

- the layout is in **portrait** or **landscape**
- they should use a particular **font**
- they should use a particular **logo**
- they should keep to certain **colours**.

Some companies only allow designers to use certain colours, and are very strict about the use of their logos. Most designers develop their own style. You can tell that some printed materials have been designed by the same designer.

Task 1

Look at **Resource 3.2 Good and bad.**

1 *Which of the slides do you prefer?*

2 *What is it that makes you like it?*

3 *What problems were there with the other slide?*

Colour schemes are chosen to suit an audience. For example, pre-school children usually like primary colours (reds, yellows and blues).

Good design balances the amount of text, images and colour with **white space**.

White space describes areas on a page that are kept plain. They allow you to pay more attention to areas where text or images have been placed. If there is too much text or too many images, then the effect is cluttered and shows poor design.

Good design includes a clear **layout** and a clear message.

Text and image effects

Computer software allows designers to add 'effects' to text and images. If used correctly then these enhance the layout, but if used incorrectly they can make it hard to read the information.

Task 2

1 Load the Paint program.

 2 Open the file **Resource 3.2 Food**.

3 Use **Image** on the Menu bar to try out some of the effects.

4 Save a new version of the image in the shared area.

 Skills help

Using image effects in Paint, page 77.

Design templates

When designers know that a design will be used regularly, for example with a monthly magazine, they will save their design layouts as template files to use again. Saving the template files with new names allows the designers to start fresh magazine work each month using the existing template. Template files can be reorganised – for example, boxes can be **resized**.

Task 3

Before developing your newsletter cover you need to review your plans from Unit 3.1 in the light of what you have learnt about good design. Work through the checklist below and make a note of anything you need to improve.

1 *Have you balanced the amount of text, images and white space?*

2 *Have you allowed space for a logo?*

3 *Have you worked out the colour scheme?*

4 *Will you be able to change things around without causing problems?*

Module Task

a Load a desktop publishing (DTP) program, for example Publisher.

b Open the file you created in Unit 3.1 and save it as a new version (put v1 after the file name) in the shared area.

c Make any changes you want to improve your design using your notes from Task 3.

d Decide on a colour scheme for the publication if you haven't already done so.

e Type in or import the text by copying and pasting into your newsletter cover.

f Import the school logo in the space you planned for the logo. Is it the right size?

g Leave spaces for images.

h Keep saving as you go along, and remember to save when you have finished.

i Print out your newsletter. Discuss with a partner the way you have both met the pointers for good design. Annotate your work to show where you would like to make further improvements.

Task 4

 *Look at **Resource 3.2 Plus and minus**.*

1 Research five logos from the Internet, newspapers and magazines.

2 Put the names of the organisations with logos that you like in the **PLUS** boxes and the names of the organisations with logos that you do not like in the **MINUS** boxes.

3 Write down the reasons for your choices.

Unit 3.3

Creating a logo

In this unit you will learn how to create an effective logo.

Why have a logo?

Why does an organisation need a logo? A logo is an important part of a corporate image. A logo is the item that can make something instantly recognisable by thousands of people.

Whose logo is this?

We all recognise certain logos even when they are not on a product of any sort.

So, a logo can be used to represent an organisation.

The look of a logo

Logos need to be versatile. For instance, an organisation might want to put one on a letterhead, business cards, websites, products, posters (large and small), or clothing. In fact, a logo could appear on any item linked to an organisation.

Effective logos are:

- clear

- able to be reproduced in colour or black and white

- simple

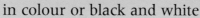

- in the company style, for example traditional or modern.

- able to be any size

How big should a logo be?

Logos have to appear in all sorts of different sizes. For this reason they are often created as **vector graphics**. Vector graphics were first discussed in Module 1 (see page 8). Using vector graphics for logos enables you to stretch and rotate them without the quality of the image being affected.

Both logos shown here are from exactly the same file. There is no difference in quality as it is enlarged.

Task 1

 Look at **Resource 3.3 Logos**.

1 Find out which companies or organisations own the logos shown. What type of organisations are they?

2 Try to find an example of each logo being used.

3 How effective do you think each logo is?

Task 2

 Look at **Resource 3.3 Places**. It contains all of the separate items needed to create a letterhead and a business card.

1 Move the items around on the first page to create the letterhead.

2 Copy the items into the second page and arrange them in the box as a business card.

3 Print off your work and save it in the shared area.

If a logo is to become well known it should be designed to last.

'Coke is coke'

'No, Coke is Coca-Cola'

Module Task

In this task you are going to create a logo for a school club, which you will use in your newsletter. You are going to use vector graphics and WordArt to create the logo.

a Load a program that will allow you to edit clip art images, for example, PowerPoint.

b Select a clip art image that you would like to form part of your logo and insert it.

c Edit the clip art image by, for example, changing the colours or rotating it.

d Use WordArt to create the title or name of your club.

e Put the image and the title together in a way that makes a strong impact. Group them together to make one graphic. Save the file with the name 'Club Logo'.

f Print out your work and annotate it to show any changes that you would like to make.

 Skills help

Creating vector graphics, page 30. (Includes help with creating grouped images. See also **Resource 3.3 Vector logos.**)

Using WordArt, page 76.

Task 3

In the next unit you will be working with images for your newsletter. Collect some examples of newsletters and magazines and write some notes on the different ways in which images are combined with the text.

Unit 3.4

Capturing images

In this unit you will learn how to capture images and manipulate them.

Images not words

Look at these magazine covers. Covers do not need to show any detail about content. They are designed to catch your attention. They do this with images representing ideas that will be expanded in one of the articles inside.

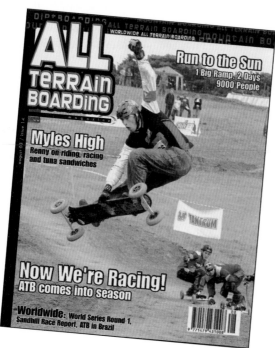

Images need to be suitable for the purpose. Designers have to make sure that the images they **import** match the design brief. The images may include logos, photographs or illustrations.

Once images have been chosen, they may need to be manipulated in some way to make them fit the design brief.

Task 1

 Look at **Resource 3.4 Articles** to help you with this task.

Record your ideas for the cover of the school newsletter.

1 *List five items that would make interesting articles for a newsletter about your school. Think about community projects, sports achievements, school clubs, teachers, school performances.*

2 *For each list, choose some words that could make headlines. Use these words to create five headlines to be used on the cover. For each headline, think of an image that would support it. Remember to include the club logo you developed in Unit 3.3.*

Capturing images

In Module 1 you may have used digital cameras and scanners to capture images for your presentation. Now you are going to capture images for your newsletter cover. Which is the best method to use?

You can be very creative with a **digital camera**, but you may need to do some preparation. Here are some things to think about.

- Will you need to visit a particular place?
- Will you need any props such as furniture or things for people to hold?
- What background/lighting will create the right atmosphere?
- What angle do you want to take the picture from – above, below, straight on?

If you get the opportunity, try out some of your ideas. Remember you can always change it if you do not like it!

Scanners are useful if you have found an ideal image in a magazine or book. Also, it is not always practical to take your own photographs. Make sure that images you want to scan are not protected by copyright (see page 10). Before you scan an image, think about whether you need all or only part of it. What will make the most impact?

Ask your teacher what format to save your images in. Some formats take up more space than others.

Manipulating images

Manipulating images means changing them. Tools for manipulating images include sizing, colours and cropping tools. This image has been:

- resized
- rotated
- colours have been changed
- and cropped.

Task 2

Load an art program, for example Paint.

Open the file **Resource 3.4 Graphics**.

This image is to be used as a logo in a magazine that comes out four times a year:

Spring   Summer
Autumn   Winter

1 Use the software tools to alter the image to suit the different seasons.

2 Save your work in the shared area.

3 Print off your work and annotate it to explain your choice of colours.

▶ *Skills help*

Working with colours in Paint, page 76.

Module Task

You are going to insert images into the front cover of your newsletter. Use your notes from Task 1 to help you decide what images you need.

a Load a desktop publishing program that allows you to import images from a digital camera or scanner, for example, Publisher.

b Open a blank document.

  c Look at **Resource 3.4 Acquiring images**.

d You should acquire one image from a digital camera and one from a scanner.

e Select **Format** to change the image colours and size, if necessary.

f Use the **Picture** toolbar to crop, rotate or resize the image if necessary.

g Select and copy the image or save it. Close the file.

h Open your school newsletter cover file and insert the image you have just created into the document. You can either paste it or insert it if you saved the image as a separate file.

i Save it as a new version of your newsletter in the shared area.

j Continue to add the rest of the images to your document in the same way.

k Keep saving and remember to save when you have finished.

 Skills help

Working with images in Publisher, page 76.

Resource 3.4 Acquiring images

Images should not be changed so much that they no longer match their purpose.

'My passport photo wasn't a very good one so I had it changed a bit.'

Task 3

1. EITHER acquire an image in an art program such as Jasc Paintshop Pro, OR load MS Paint and insert one of the images you used in the Module Task.

2. Use a range of the tools to enhance the image, for example you could work with a limited colour range or you could add an **Effect**.

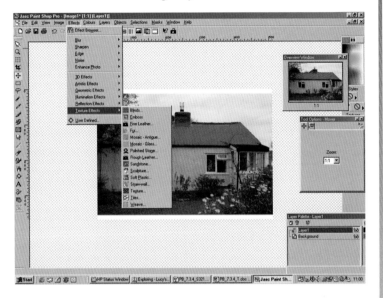

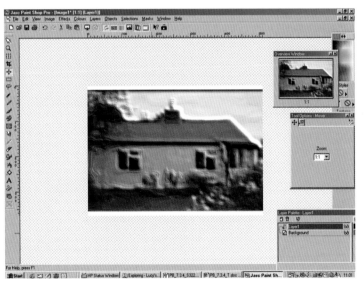

3. Save the image to the shared area.

4. If you used an image from your newsletter cover, import the new version back into your newsletter and save the latest version of your work.

Task 4

The school has decided to produce a two-sided A4 leaflet to send out to parents of children who may want to join the school next year. It should have the same corporate image as the school newsletter, and re-use as much as possible of the material (text and images) from the newsletter.

1. Plan out a design for pages 1 and 2 of the leaflet.

2. Which elements will you need to re-use to ensure that the corporate image is the same. What might you have to do to them?

3. Make a list of the items you need to add to your work to turn it into a leaflet. Remember – logos and images can appear more than once!

 *Skills help*

Effects in other art programs, page 77.

Where do images come from?

So far you have used various different ways to create and acquire images.

Each way has advantages and disadvantages.

- A journalist relies on a camera for getting the images to support news articles. They need to be clear and accurate representations.

- A designer uses a combination of digital camera, scanner and software to create and manipulate images in order to produce a range of effects.

- A student can use a combination of sources, like the designer. A student can also use images that have already been created, for example clip art.

Improving images

If the design brief changes, images may need to be manipulated again before they fit the new design brief.

In Unit 3.4 you created and acquired a series of images for the newsletter. You are now going to re-use them for the two-page leaflet. The quality of these images needs to be checked before you can use them in the new leaflet.

Task 1

1 How could you make use of the different ways of creating images within your school life?

2 What are the advantages and disadvantages to you of the different ways?

Task 2

 Look at **Resource 3.5 Quality**.

1 What is wrong with one of the images?

2 What has caused it?

3 Could it be improved? How?

Module Task

You are going to develop your single-sheet newsletter cover into a two-page leaflet with a front and a back.

a *Open your newsletter document. Insert two new pages after the first one.*

b *Save the document with a new file name in the shared area.*

c *Set up the new pages with the design that you have worked out for your leaflet. Use the same margins.*

d *Copy and paste any items you need from the newsletter to create the leaflet. Think about it! To make the leaflet look different, you can:*

- resize an image

- enlarge text or change it by rotating WordArt text.

- change the colours
- crop images

e *When you have transferred everything you need to the leaflet, delete the first (original) page so you have a two-page document.*

f *Keep saving as you go along, and remember to save when you have finished.*

▶ *Skills help*

Adding pages in a document in Publisher, pages 74–75.

Setting margins in a document in Publisher, page 74.

Task 3

The information leaflet you created in the Module Task is to have a tear-off strip at the bottom for people to contact the school for more information.

1 *What are the details that need to be included?*

2 *What features are normally used in a tear-off strip?*

3 *Create a suitable area on the second page of your leaflet and set it up as a tear-off strip.*

4 *Save the latest version of your work to the shared area.*

Task 4

 *Look at **Resource 3.5 Process**.*

In this module you have been through the whole process of developing a newsletter and a leaflet. Write a description of the stages of the development:

1 *What was the initial design brief? How did it change?*

2 *How did you work out the corporate image?*

3 *How did you develop the logo for your club?*

4 *How did you get the images? What did you do to them?*

5 *List any three things that you like about your leaflet.*

6 *List the changes that you would make to the way you worked if you had to create another leaflet.*

Unit 3.6
Creating a folded leaflet

In this unit you will learn how to transfer items between documents with different layouts.

Layout of leaflets

Leaflets are an ideal way of communicating a lot of information to reach a big audience.

Some of the most popular layouts of leaflets are:

- one-fold
- two-fold
- single-sheet
- fancy-fold, for special presentations.

Task 1

 Look at **Resource 3.6 Folds**.

1 Which shapes would create a:
   - single-sheet leaflet
   - one-fold leaflet
   - zigzag two-fold leaflet
   - fancy-fold leaflet.

2 Print the file. Cut out the shapes and fold the paper along the lines to find out how they could be used.

3 What problems would the folds cause for design work?

Front and back

A folded leaflet has a number of different sections that are together on the same side of a sheet of paper, so the design layout has to be worked out carefully. There are different ways of folding a sheet of paper to make a one-fold leaflet.

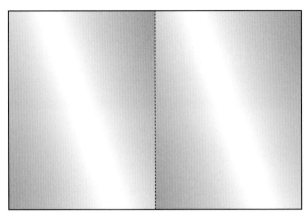

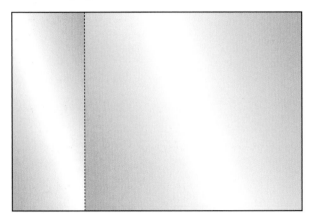

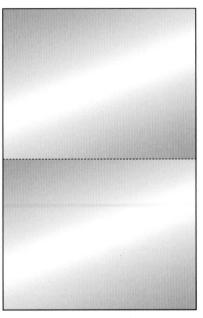

For each of these the layout of text and images would need to be different. Remember that each page has a front and a back!

Task 2

 Look at **Resource 3.6 Overlap**.

The file has been set up to be a one-fold document. This means it is a piece of A4 paper folded in half lengthways, and printed on both sides, so it has four long, thin pages. You can see the front of the leaflet when you open the file.

1 Place the three images onto the leaflet.

2 Try them in different places to see what the effect would be on them when the paper is folded. Where do they look best?

3 When you are satisfied with the layout, print out the leaflet, fold it and see what happens.

N.B. Your printer will only print one side of the paper, so you will end up with two A4 sheets, which you need to stick back-to-back..

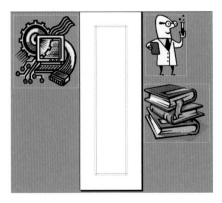

4 Annotate the leaflet to show why you have chosen the places for the images

Module Task

You are now going to change your two-page leaflet into a one-fold leaflet. You will be changing the **format** of the document. You have all the images, text and layout ideas already. The aim is to present the same information in a different way. You will work within one document and **transfer** information between pages.

a Open your two-page leaflet. Add in two new pages. These will become the new leaflet when you have finished.

b Make sure the page setup is correct for the type of leaflet that you want to design. You may need to change margins, or move from portrait to landscape.

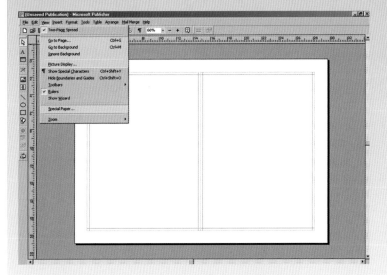

c Save this file with a new file name in the shared area.

d Select items from your previous leaflet and transfer them one at a time to new positions on the folded leaflet.

e Make changes to each item as necessary and keep looking at the overall layout of the pages. Remember they are going to be folded.

f When you have transferred everything you need to the folded leaflet pages, delete the original two pages.

g Keep saving as you go along, and remember to save the final version.

h Print out your folded leaflet.

 *Skills help*

Setting up page layout in a Publisher document, pages 73–4.

Task 3

The leaflet needs to have more information and will become a two-fold leaflet.

1 Follow the same prodecure as in the Module Task to turn your leaflet into a two-fold leaflet. If you do not have enough information to fill a two-fold leaflet, leave the back panel blank.

Task 4

This module has helped you to understand how to set up different types of publications.

1 What are the key points for developing leaflets?

2 Write down three key points that you think are essential to know before you start design work.

3 Write down a list of the key words that you think are important for good design.

4 Write down a list of the key words that you think give a good finish to a document.

Leisure centre

To complete Module 3 you are to produce a leaflet.

Background

A leisure centre at the North Gwylfa Arena in Hayburgh, North Cheshire, is about to open a new facility – a swimming pool. This promises to offer a new and exciting amenity to local residents.

The new facility is a swimming pool with:

- flumes
- a wave machine
- interactive fountains
- special effects – Caribbean and the tropics.

Activities in the pool include:

- aqua-aerobics
- swimming classes: under 5s
    5–9 years
    intermediate
    advanced
    senior
    adult
    over 50s
- childrens' parties
- theme evenings.

Opening hours are:

Mon – Fri   6.30am – 10.00pm
Sat, Sun   10.00pm – 6.00pm
Extensions for 'Theme evenings'

Images can be taken from the Image Bank in the shared area or you can find your own.

Use the knowledge you have gained from all of the units in this module to help you to create a leaflet for the leisure centre.

Plan carefully!

Brief

You are to produce a two-fold leaflet to introduce the new facility. This will be sent to all local residents.

Your leaflet should include a corporate image, with:

- a logo
- images – photographs and clip art
- text.

Remember the process you followed:

- corporate image
- logos
- images
- text.

Some of the skills you need in this module are covered in Module 1 Skills help: in particular the use of vector graphics and grouping objects. For help with these things please see page 30.

Setting up a document in MS Publisher

The following instructions all refer to Publisher. If you are using a different DTP program, similar concepts and commands will be found to do the same things.

Load Publisher. If a catalogue appears on the screen, click **Cancel**. A blank document will appear.

The document shows you where the margins have been set and the orientation – either portrait or landscape. This one is set to portrait.

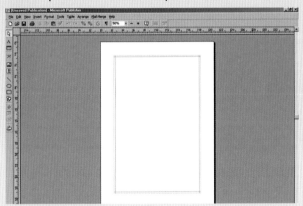

Creating a new document

If you are already in the program and you want to start a new document, click **File**, **New** on the **Menu** bar. A new blank document will appear.

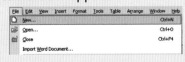

Saving a document

Click **File**, **Save**. If this is the first time you have saved the document, you will need to type in a name for the document in the **File name** box and click **OK**.

Changing the page orientation

1   Click on **File**, **Page Setup**. A dialogue box appears.

2   Choose the orientation that you want – landscape or portrait.

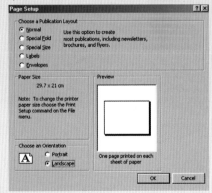

You can also use this dialogue box to set up special publication layouts.

Setting margins and grid guides

1 Click on **Arrange**, **Layout Guides**. A dialogue box appears.

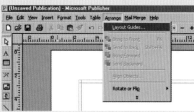

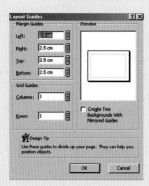

2 In the **Margin Guides** box you can adjust the margins for your document. This will increase or decrease the overall work area that you have. The preview window shows what the new margins will look like.

3 In the **Grid Guides** box you can adjust the number of columns or rows that you want.

● This shows 2 columns and 1 row. It splits the page in half vertically.

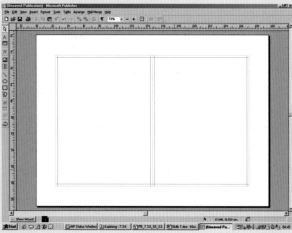

● If you set it the other way – 1 column and 2 rows – the layout looks like this.

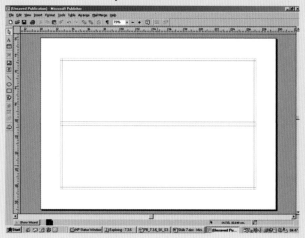

It splits it horizontally.

● You can make as many columns and rows as you need to help you with a design.

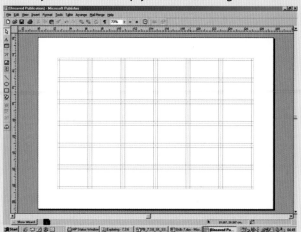

Adding more pages to your document

1 Click on **Insert**, **Page**. A dialogue box appears.

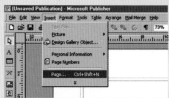

2 Choose the number of pages that you want to add and whether they should come before or after the page you are working on.

3 At the bottom left of the screen a row of little page shapes shows how many pages are currently in the document. You will see new ones appear when you add pages. The page that you are working on is coloured black. In this example, the current page is page 3 of the document.

Adding text to Publisher

There are two ways that text can be added:

Text frames

1 Click on the **Text Frame** icon on the tool bar.

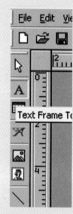

2 Click and drag out a frame to the size that you want.

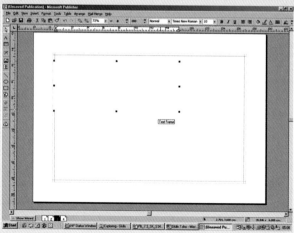

3 Click in the frame and type in your text. By highlighting the text you can change it as in a word-processing program.

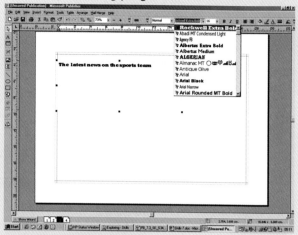

To delete a text frame:

4 Right click on the text frame you wish to delete.

5 Click on **Delete Object**.

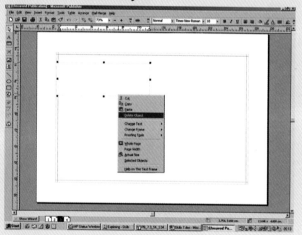

Layering frames

Text and picture frames can be layered one on top of the other.

1 Click on the frame you want to move.

2 Click on **Arrange, Order**.

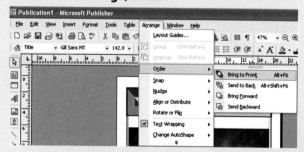

3 Click on whichever movement you want the frame to make – bring to front or send to back.

Word Art

1 Click on the **Word Art Frame** icon from the tool bar.

2 A different screen appears. This is the Word Art screen. You can select the style and the shape of the words that you enter into the text box.

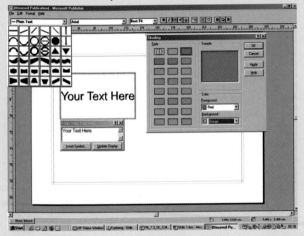

3 The Word Art Text Frame can be moved about on screen by clicking and dragging.

Working with images in Publisher

Resizing images

1 Click on the image you wish to resize.
2 Click on one of the handles and drag until the image is the size that you want. To keep the proportions the same, use the corner handles only.

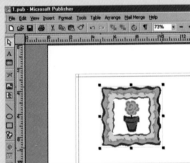

Changing image colours

1 Click on **Format**, **Recolour Picture**. A dialogue box opens.
2 Click on the down arrow by Colour and the colour menu opens.
3 Select the colour that you would like for the image.

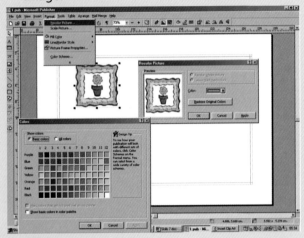

Using MS Paint

Working with colours

1 Click on **Edit Colours**, **Define Custom Colours**.
2 Click on a white box under **Custom Colour**. Select a colour from the colour palette on the right.
3 Click on **Add to Custom Colour**. The new colour will then be available for you to use in your work.

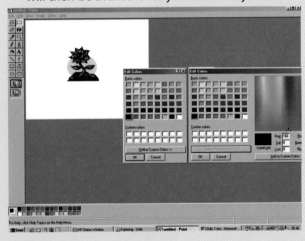

Working with image effects

There are various other special effects which you can access by clicking **Image** on the main **Menu** bar and choosing options from the drop-down menu. In this example, the **Invert Colour** option has been chosen.

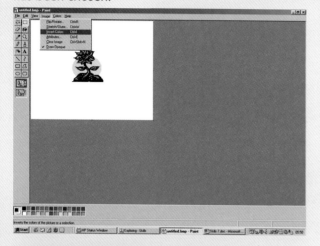

You might want to try out some of the other effects.

Effects in other art programs

Within some art programs, for example Jasc PaintShop Pro, there are tools that allow effects to be added to images. In the image below, the **Effects** tools have allowed sections of the baby's face to be altered.

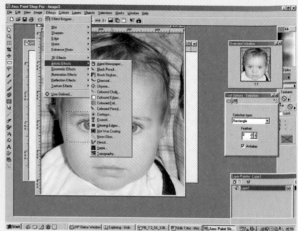

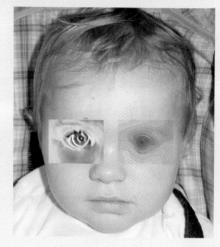

Why not experiment with the software you have?

In this module you will learn how to set up a spreadsheet as a **model** of a real life situation.

Before you start there are some skills and words that you will need to know. Read about each skill in the boxes below and then decide which of the following statements best describes how you feel about it:

A I am confident that I understand / can do this.
B I think I understand / can do this, but I would like to check.
C I definitely don't know how to do this and I need to learn.

Using spreadsheet software

A spreadsheet is like a table drawn out on the computer screen. The table is made up of **cells**. The cells are in **rows** and **columns**. Each cell has a unique **cell reference**. The rows and columns all have labels.

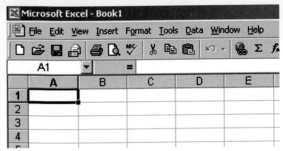

Labels. To know which column or row you are looking at, there is a label at the top or the side. These are 1, 2, 3, 4 or A, B, C, D.

Cells. These are the smallest part of the spreadsheet. They are the 'boxes' that data is entered into.

Rows. These are numbered from the top to the bottom of a spreadsheet with 1 at the top.

Columns. These are labelled A, B, C and so on across the spreadsheet.

Cell reference. This tells you where a cell is. Cell A1 is in the first column and the first row. Cell C12 is in the third column and the 12th row.

Entering data into a spreadsheet

Data is typed into the cells of a spreadsheet. It can be **text**, **variables** or a **formula**.

Text. This is letters and characters; the labels for column titles or names of things.

Variables. These are numbers that are entered into a cell.

Formulas. These are used in spreadsheets to carry out calculations.

They always start with an = sign.
+ means add
- means subtract
* means multiply
/ means divide.

Creating graphs/charts in a spreadsheet

The data entered into a spreadsheet can be used to create charts, which display the information graphically. There are different sorts of charts and graphs used to display the data as clearly as possible, for example **column charts** and **line graphs**. If the data is edited, the graph will change automatically.

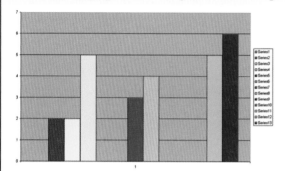

Column chart. This represents data in columns. It makes it easy to compare the values of the data in a spreadsheet file.

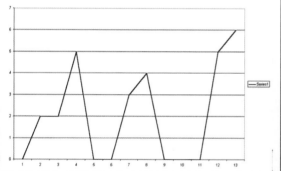

Line graph. This represents data by a number of points joined together to make a line. It is easy to see **trends** in a line graph.

Trends. These show whether values are increasing or decreasing.

Task

 Open **Resource 4 Circus takings**.

1 Write down the number which appears in cell B3. What type of data is this?

2 Change the number in cell B5 to 600. What happens to the number in cell D5?

3 Write down the formula in cell D4. What does it calculate?

4 What type of data is in the cells in row 1?

5 Write down the cell reference of the formula that calculates the total of all the items sold for the week.

6 What type of chart has been used to show this data?

Using a spreadsheet

What is a spreadsheet?

A spreadsheet is a piece of software which can perform a large number of calculations at the same time. It is a table made up of **cells** arranged in **rows** and **columns**. Examples of spreadsheet software are MS Excel or Lotus 1, 2, 3.

Spreadsheets are used when calculations are to be carried out again and again. They can process things very quickly and when a spreadsheet has been set up it can be used many times. **Graphs** and **charts** can be produced from data in a spreadsheet.

Task 1

 Look at **Resource 4.1 Show stoppers**, which shows the table opposite. It gives bookings for stage shows that a group of students are going to see.

1 Work out the total cost of all the tickets. Look at the table if you need some help with the sums you need to do.

2 Will they have any money left in the budget?

 Now look at **Resource 4.1 Shows.**

3 This spreadsheet has been set up to do the same calculations as you have just done. Check to see whether your results are the same.

4 Click on each of the cells in column H. Look at the formulas which appear in the formula bar to see how the spreadsheet works out the sums.

Total cost = Ticket price × amount needed

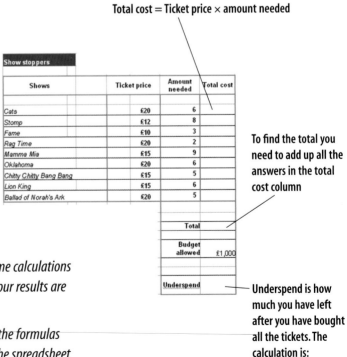

Show stoppers				
Shows		Ticket price	Amount needed	Total cost
Cats		£20	6	
Stomp		£12	8	
Fame		£10	3	
Rag Time		£20	2	
Mamma Mia		£15	9	
Oklahoma		£20	6	
Chitty Chitty Bang Bang		£15	5	
Lion King		£15	6	
Ballad of Norah's Ark		£20	5	
			Total	
			Budget allowed	£1,000
			Underspend	

To find the total you need to add up all the answers in the total cost column

Underspend is how much you have left after you have bought all the tickets. The calculation is: Budget – Total

Using formulas

Formulas are used to tell the computer to carry out a calculation. You always type the formula in the cell where you want the answer to appear.

If you wanted a spreadsheet to calculate the answer to $20 \div 5$, you could type in the formula =20/5. The formula would appear in the formula bar, and the answer, 4, would appear in the cell.

Often it is better to show the numbers you are using in your calculation, and have the answer appear in a separate cell. In that case you would need to use **cell references** in your formula and your spreadsheet might look something like this:

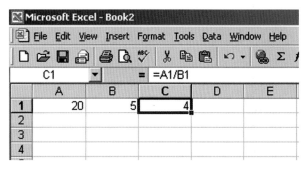

The formula in cell C1 is =A1/B1. It tells the computer to divide whatever number is in cell A1 by whatever number is in B1. If you decided that actually you wanted to divide 20 by 10, all you would need to do is alter the number in cell B1 from 5 to 10. The formula wouldn't need to change. The numbers in cells A1 and B1 are called **variables** – because you can vary them and see what different answers you come up with.

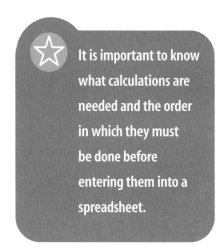

It is important to know what calculations are needed and the order in which they must be done before entering them into a spreadsheet.

Everything is relative

Often in spreadsheets it is necessary to do the same calculation on a range of different variables. An example is the 'Show stoppers' spreadsheet you looked at in Task 1.

In cell H6 the formula =F6*G6 calculates the number of tickets in cell F6 multiplied by the price in cell G6.

The formula in cell H7 is =F7*G7. The software automatically uses the numbers from line 7 instead of line 6.

If you are setting up a spreadsheet you can enter a formula once and then copy and paste it as many times as you want down the column. The spreadsheet will automatically use the variables from each new line. This is called **relative cell referencing**.

A quick way of copying formulas down a column is to use a software tool called the **fill handle**. This tool can also be used to insert numbers and some text in sequences far quicker than typing them in or writing them out.

Skills help

Using the fill handle in Excel, page 107.

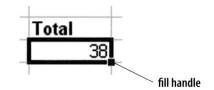

fill handle

Task 2

 Look at **Resource 4.1 Calendar**.

This is the calendar for 2003. The 1st of January was on a Wednesday.

1 Use the fill handle tool to add the days of the week and dates for the other months.

2 Could you write them out that quickly?

'Look, I've set up an automated calender for the whole of the year'.

It all adds up

In the 'Show stoppers' spreadsheet the formula in cell H17 adds up the total of all the answers in cells H6 to H14. This is a very common type of calculation used in spreadsheets. There are several ways it can be done:

You could type in the formula =H6+H7+H8… etc. It might be a very long formula!

'That's great Ben… but do you know anyone who has a birthday on the 30th February?'

A quicker formula is =SUM(H6:H14) . This means 'add up all the numbers in cells H6 to H14'.

An even quicker way is to use the AutoSum button.

Highlight all the cells you want to add up, plus the empty cell in which you want the answer to appear, then click the Auto Sum button.

▶ *Skills help*

Saving an Excel spreadsheet with a new filename, page 103.

Entering data in Excel, page 105.

Copying, and pasting in Excel, pages 106–7.

Using formulas in Excel, page 107.

Module Task

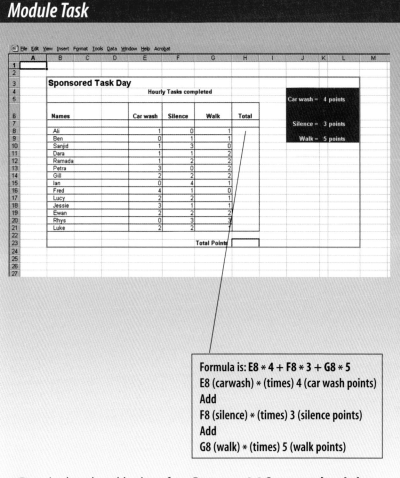

Formula is: E8 * 4 + F8 * 3 + G8 * 5
E8 (carwash) * (times) 4 (car wash points)
Add
F8 (silence) * (times) 3 (silence points)
Add
G8 (walk) * (times) 5 (walk points)

🖰 *Look at the table above from **Resource 4.1 Sponsored task day**. It shows a record of a Sponsored Task Day where groups of pupils carried out tasks to earn points.*

a Look at the illustration to see what the formula is to calculate the total number of points gained by Ali.

b Write down the formula you would need to enter in cell H9 to calculate the total number of points gained by Ben.

c Write down the formula to calculate Sanjid's total points. Where would you enter that formula?

d Write down a formula you could enter in cell H23 to calculate the total number of points gained by everyone added together. How many different ways of calculating this sum can you think of?

🖰 *Look at **Resource 4.1 Sponsors**. Save it with your own filename in the shared area.*

e Type in the formulas you have worked out into the cells H8, H9, H10 and H23.

f Use copy and paste or the fill handle to enter formulas to calculate all the other pupils' totals in cells H11 to H21.

g What is the total in cell (H23) when you have finished all this?

h Save and print your spreadsheet.

Task 3

 Look at **Resource 4.1 Extra**.

1 What type of data is held in cells K5, K7 and K9 (text, variable or formula)?

2 Look at the formula in cell H8. What is the difference between this formula and the one you used in cell H8 in the Module Task?

3 Can you think of any advantages in using this formula instead of the other one?

4 What does the $ sign mean when it is used in formulas?

5 Look at **Resource 4.1 Using absolute cell references** if you need help with this task.

▶ Skills help

Absolute cell referencing in Excel, page 107.

See also **Resource 4.1 Using absolute cell references**

Task 4

1 Make a list of the advantages of using a spreadsheet to do calculations.

2 Write down any possible disadvantages you can think of.

Unit 4.2

Modelling using a spreadsheet

In this unit you will learn what a model is and how to use a model to find information and to answer 'what if?' questions.

What is a model?

A **model** is a simulation of a real-life situation. Models are often used to predict the effects of possible changes in a situation.

Many models are to do with money. For example, a model could be created to work out how savings would increase if left in a bank account and compare this with how much they would grow if they were invested in stocks and shares.

Emergency services use models to simulate what could happen in real emergencies.

Models are also used to **simulate** dangerous real-life situations. Powerful computers are used to create simulations of what might happen in emergencies, allowing emergency services to plan well ahead for potential problems.

Sorting data

Sometimes the information in a model can be difficult to see because it is all jumbled up. Spreadsheets can help with this because it is very easy to sort cell content into highest, lowest and a range of values in the middle.

To **sort data** you select the columns of data that you want sorted and use the **Sort** feature that is on the **Data** menu in Excel, for example.

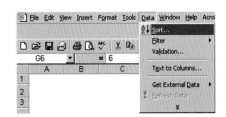

Task 1

 Look at **Resource 4.2 Groups** and **Resource 4.2 Sorting**.

1 Use **Sort** to find out:

- who has highest score in each group?
- who has lowest score in each group?
- which Group has most scores over 20?
- which Group has most scores under 10?

2 Write down your answers.

3 Close the file.

 Skills help

Using Sort in Excel, page 137.

Using a model to answer 'What if?' questions

It is very easy to change **variables** in a spreadsheet and see what the effect is. For this reason, models are used to try and answer 'What if?' questions.

Look at the case study opposite. Models are used every day to answer these kinds of life or death questions. The different possibilities are sometimes called **scenarios**.

Case study

There is an epidemic in a city. The disease is spreading quickly. Already there are 400 people in hospital and 50 new cases every day. There are 2 hospitals, each with 1000 beds. How long will it be before they are full? What if each hospital could cram in an extra 10% more beds, how many more days would it be before they were full? What if the rate of new cases increases?

Task 2

 Look at **Resource 4.2 Show more**.

Use this model to work out what would happen in each of these 'What if?' scenarios.

1 What if you only had a budget of £500 and you could only make bookings for five shows?

2 What if the budget was £1000 but seats for Chitty Chitty Bang Bang and Fame went up to £20 each?

3 What if your budget was £1000, but Cats was cancelled and the people who had selected to go to Cats had to transfer to another show?

 For help with this task, look at **Resource 4.2 What if**.

Structure of a model

All models consist of **inputs**, **rules** and **outputs**. The table below shows how spreadsheets are used to make models.

	What this means	What it looks like in a spreadsheet	Effects of changing it
Inputs	The things you know about before you start	The numbers or variables which you input	Can be changed within a model to see what happens
Rules	What the model can and cannot do	The calculations (written as formulas)	If you change the rules the model changes
Outputs	What happens when you apply the rules	The answers to the calculations	Will change if either the inputs or the rules are changed

Module Task

 *Open **Resource 4.2 Updates** and save it with your own file name in the shared area.*

	A	B	C	D	E	F	G	H	I	J	K	L
1												
2												
3		Sponsored Task Day										
4						Hourly Tasks completed						
5										Car wash =		4 points
6		Names			Car wash	Silence	Walk	Total				
7										Silence =		3 points
8		Ali			1	0	1	9				
9		Ben			0	1	1	8		Walk =		5 points
10		Sanjid			1	3	0	13				
11		Dara			1	1	2	17				
12		Ramada			1	2	2	20		Updated Point scores		
13		Petra			3	0	2	22				
14		Gill			2	2	2	24		Car wash	5 points	
15		Ian			0	4	1	17		Silence	4 points	
16		Fred			4	1	0	19		Walk	6 points	
17		Lucy			2	2	1	19				
18		Jessie			3	1	1	20		Litter collect	5 points	
19		Ewan			2	2	2	24				
20		Rhys			0	3	3	24				
21		Luke			2	2	1	19				
22												
23							Total Points	255				

You are going to look at a 'What if' scenario for the Sponsored Task Day. The number of points available for each of the activities has changed. The new points are:

Car wash = 5 points
Silence = 8 points
Walk = 6 points

a *Update the formulas in column H using the new point scores. Remember that you can copy formulas down the column.*

b *There are actually five different groups doing the Sponsored Task Day. Click on the **Groups** tab to open a second worksheet showing the totals for each of the five groups.*

c *Update the Groups Table with the new totals for Group 1 which you have just calculated.*

d *Sort each Group's results in descending order with the highest score at the top. Print this page and compare the results with your printout from Task 1. Which group now has the most points over 20?*

e *Save your file.*

Task 3

1 Open the 'Updates' file you worked on in the Module Task and save it with a new file name.

2 Change the formulas in column H reflect to the new point scores, using absolute cell references.

3 A new task has been added – Litter collection – worth 6 points. Add a new column called Litter. Enter some data for each person for litter collection – you can make up the data.

4 Update the formulas in column H so that litter collection is also added to each person's total.

5 Save and print out your work.

 Skills help

Adding columns in Excel, page 104.

Absolute cell referencing in Excel, page 107.

See also **Resource 4.1 Using absolute cell references**.

Task 4

 Look at **Resource 4.2 Planning a model**.

1 What are the three main elements of a model?

2 If you were creating your own spreadsheet model from scratch, what do you think you would need to do first?

3 What kinds of things would you need to work out away from a computer and what should you do at the machine?

Unit **4.3**

In this unit you will create a spreadsheet model of a situation.

Building a model

Setting the ground rules

To design a model you have to work out exactly what you want it to do. It will work according to the rules that you set up.

In a spreadsheet model, the rules are expressed in terms of calculations or sums which are written as **formulas**.

The outcomes or answers which your model produces depend on the variables or numbers which you put into it.

When these things have been worked out, then the way the model will look can be considered. Good presentation can make a model easier to use.

A good model can be easily altered and updated.

Task 1

 Look at **Resource 4.3 Rules** and **Resource 4.3 Design**.

1 Look at the way the spreadsheet has been set out.
  a What needs to happen to make it work?
  b What formulas are needed and where should they be?
  c What variables are needed and where would they come from?

2 Write down your answers.

3 Close the file.

	Points Earned	
	Monday	
Group 1		
Group 2		
Group 3		
Group 4		
Group 5		
Total Points		
Sponsors rate	£0.50	
Total £		
School Costs	£10	
Total income		

Creating formulas

It is important to know how to translate a rule into a formula. Here are some commonly used rules and the formulas used to express them.

Rule	Formula
Calculate the <u>total value</u> of a list of variables.	You need to <u>add up</u> all the variables involved. You can do this in several ways: =A2+B2+C2+D2 =SUM(A2:D2) or by highlighting the numbers to be added and using the auto-sum button
Calculate the <u>difference</u> between two variables. This is often used to work out if you are over or under a set budget. Remember, the answer may be a minus figure!	Take one variable away from the other one: =A2-A3
Calculate the <u>total cost</u>, when you know the price and you know how many you want. This rule is used whenever there is a <u>rate per unit</u> of something, e.g. hours per day, price per unit, output per person, etc.	<u>Multiply</u> the price by the number you want to buy. For example: =£5.00*25 More generally this can be thought of as: =unit rate*number of units
Show the <u>proportion</u> of the total which this figure represents.	<u>Divide</u> the figure by the total: =A2/A10 The answer is often shown as a percentage.

Task 2

 Open **Resource 4.3 Day**, and save the file with your own file name in the shared area.

The Sponsored Task Day is one day in a series of sponsored task days under a Sponsor Scheme. In this task you will complete a model which will calculate the income from one day of the scheme. This means the total amount of money earned.

1 *Using your notes from Task 1 as a reference, copy and paste the variables that you need from the Groups worksheet into the correct places on the Daily Total worksheet.*
2 *Enter the formulas that you worked out for the calculations that are needed.*
3 *Are the results sensible? Compare your answers with your partner's.*
4 *Make any changes you want to and then save your work.*

Presentation

Good presentation is important because it makes the model clear and easy to use. In particular, the user needs to know what type of information is in each cell.

- Is it a label?
- Is it a total or one of a list?
- Is it a date?
- Is it money? If so, what currency is it?
- Is it a percentage or an actual figure?
- Which is the most important information on this worksheet?

The formatting menu allows you to **format** (or present) numbers as dates, currency and percentages.

You can also use font size and style, bold, italic, and colour backgrounds and borders to make your model easier to use.

 Skills help

Formatting cells in Excel, pages 105–6.

Using **Fill Down** and **Fill Right** in Excel, page 107.

Task 3

 *Look at **Resource 4.3 Framed**. This model is used by a company that sells framed pictures. It has been developed in three stages:*

Stage 1 *(Formulas tab) The rules have been decided*
Stage 2 *(Layout tab) The basic layout and formatting of cells have been decided*
Stage 3 *(Final tab) Colour and images have been added to make it look attractive*

1 *Click on the **Formulas** tab. Which cells contain formulas? What do you think are the rules for this model?*

2 *Click on the **Layout** tab. Make notes about the features that make it look different. For example, the types of fonts, number formats, alignment, cell width, font styles that have been used. Why do you think these changes have been made?*

3 *Click on the **Final** tab. What additional changes have been made? Do they make the model easier or more difficult to use? Are they necessary?*

Module Task

 *Open **Resource 4.3 Week**, and save it with your own file name in the shared area.*

In Task 2 you developed a layout for a one-day model which calculated the total income from one day of the Sponsor Scheme. That same layout is shown under the column heading 'Monday' in this worksheet. You are now going to add in data for the other days of the week and work out a 5 Day Total.

1 *Enter your data from Task 2 in the 'Monday' column.*

2 *Click on the **Group Totals** tab to see the data for the rest of the week for each group.*

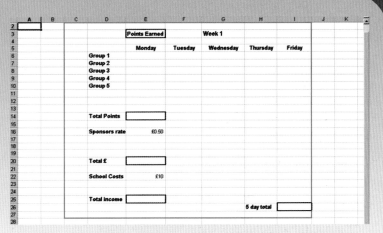

3 *Copy and paste the data for Tuesday to Friday into the 5 Day Total worksheet.*

4 *Use the Fill Down and Fill Right Menus to copy the formulas across where you can.*

5 *What formula do you need to get the 5 Day Total? Enter it into cell I26.*

6 *Save and print out your work.*

Flexibility of models

A model can be used many times to try out different 'What if?' scenarios. Usually only one or two variables need to be changed each time. Sometimes the cells containing the variables which can be altered are highlighted – perhaps with a different colour or font – in order to make them stand out.

Show stoppers			
Shows	Ticket price	Amount needed	Total cost
Cats	£20	6	£120
Stomp	£12	8	£96
Fame	£10	3	£30
Rag Time	£20	2	£40
Mamma Mia	£15	9	£135
Oklahoma	£20	6	£120
Chitty Chitty Bang Bang	£15	5	£75
Lion King	£15	6	£90
Ballad of Norah's Ark	£20	5	£100
		Total	£806
		Budget allowed	£1,000
		Underspend	£194

Task 4

Two changes happen during the time that the Sponsor Scheme is running.

Change 1: A new sponsor joins the scheme and is going to offer £1.00 per point for the two highest scoring days of the week.

1 *What changes are needed to the model to include this sponsor? Clue: you will need to change some formulas as well as variables.*

2 *Open the latest version of your sponsor model and add in Sponsor 2 at a rate of £1.00 per point on the two highest scoring days.*

3 *Make the necessary changes to the formulas.*

4 *Save your work in the shared area.*

Change 2: The school has had to put its daily charge up to £15 per day.

5 *Make the change to the spreadsheet and apply it to all of the days.*

6 *Save this as a different version of the file in the shared area.*

7 *Is the scheme making more money after the changes?*

Task 5

1 *Identify any problems there could be in using the model for additional weeks of the Sponsor Scheme.*

2 *Is there any better way of carrying out the calculations in other weeks to save a lot of copying and pasting of data?*

Unit 4.4
Refining and developing a model

In this unit you will learn how to refine your model and add more variables to it.

Changing rules

One important feature of a spreadsheet model is that it can easily be changed to cope with different situations. Spreadsheet models are set up to answer 'What if?' questions. As we can never be sure what these questions might be, the model has to be flexible enough to cope with changes in the rules as well as just changes to variables.

Financial news often tells of interest rates going up and going down.

When changes happen, financial organisations do not have to start from the beginning again. Their financial models are set up so that changing a single variable will alter the financial forecasts.

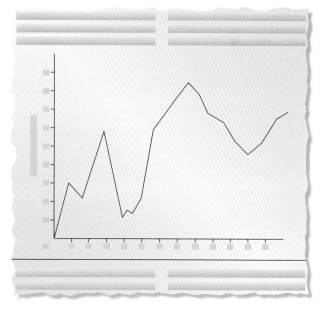

Stock market models are changing all the time.

Stock markets make use of models to project what they should do with shares. The rules they use change by the minute, so the models that they use have to be very efficient and fast for them to make profits.

Task 1

The rules for the Sponsor Scheme are changing.

NEW RULES

- The Sponsor Scheme is now going to be run over four weeks, seven days a week.

- To encourage more people to join, everyone who takes part will get a T-shirt.

- A T-shirt will cost the scheme £0.80 if they order more than 250. If they order up to 250 T-shirts they will cost £1.00 each.

- They are going to limit the number of groups that can take part to ten in any one week – each group will still have no more than 14 people in it.

- Groups can not take part more than once.

- The school has decided that each week it will give a mug to each member of the group that scores the most points.

- The mugs cost the scheme £1.50 each.

1 What is this going to do to the weekly model that you have got?

2 How will it affect the costs and the profits made at the end of each week?

3 What new formulas will be needed?

4 How will you set them up?

 Use **Resource 4.4 New rules** to help you to plan out the changes that you will have to make to the model.

Checking models

'I'd always thought about modelling, you know'

When changes are made to a model it is important to check that formulas (old as well as new) are still working properly. A good way to do this is to enter some test data into the model. Instead of the real numbers, use very easy numbers such as 1 or 10 so that you can quickly see whether the formulas are working properly. When you are testing a model, it is a good idea to test only one thing at a time.

As models become more complicated, it is sometimes useful to have a test copy of the model on a separate page on which you can try things out. To make a test copy, add another page, or worksheet, to your model. Make a copy of the entire model and paste it into the new worksheet. The new worksheet can be named as 'Testing' to make it clear which one has the real model. Worksheets added to a model will not affect the actual model.

Open your sponsor model file 5 Day version. You are going to use some test data to check that the formulas are still correct following the changes you made in Unit 4.3.

1 Add an extra worksheet to the file. Rename the new worksheet 'Testing' by double clicking on the tab at the bottom of the screen. Make a copy of the model and paste it onto the Testing page.

2 On the Testing version of the model delete the actual points scored and type in some test data.

3 Check the results which appear in the formula cells. Are they what you expected? If not, then ask a partner if they can see what is going wrong and work out a better solution together.

4 If necessary, update the formulas in the main model in the light of what you have found out on your testing page. Save your work.

▶ *Skills help*

Copying an entire worksheet in Excel, pages 103–4.

Inserting and naming a new worksheet in Excel, page 104.

> ☆ **When you are testing a model you will only know whether it is correct or not if you have some idea of the answers you are expecting it to give.**

Predicting outcomes

Sometimes past experience can help us to predict possible outcomes of a model. Let's take another look at the epidemic case study we looked at in Unit 4.2.

Case study

The modellers know that in the last epidemic the daily rate of new cases was like this:

Week 1	30	Week 5	92
Week 2	67	Week 6	70
Week 3	81	Week 7	44
Week 4	103	Week 8	29

Using these figures they can predict how the new epidemic will develop if it follows a similar pattern. They can also try different scenarios – what if it turns out to be twice as bad or half as bad as last time? The past experience gives them a sensible starting point for predicting possible outcomes of this epidemic.

Module Task

Look at **Resource 4.4 Changes**.

		Points earned		Week 1					
		Monday	**Tuesday**	**Wednesday**	**Thursday**	**Friday**	**Saturday**	**Sunday**
Group 1		235	235	245	220	210	135	125
Group 2		220	0	0	220	210	210	85
Group 3		240	250	210	218	215	245	230
Group 4		0	210	0	240	230	200	0
Group 5		245	225	235	235	210	240	230
Group 6		220	235	210	210	210	120	218
Group 7		35	240	0	210	180	195	0
Group 8		140	218	215	200	240	240	210
Group 9		120	200	218	0	120	140	220
Group 10		240	0	240	240	0	150	200
Total points								
Total number of people this week		124						
Sponsors rate		£0.50						
Total income £				**Highest points =**				
School costs		£10						
T-shirts cost								
Mugs cost								
Total costs								
Net income							**Total points**	

a Check your plan from Task 1 against this example. There are comments in some of the cells to help you get the rules correct. Make notes on your planning sheet and correct any mistakes.

b Minimise the 'Changes' file and open the latest version of your sponsor model file. Save it with a new file name, such as 'Sponsors 7 Day Model'.

c Using the planning notes you have made, change your model so that it works like the 'Changes' file, for Week 1.

d When you think your model is correct, enter some simple test data and check that all the formulas work. Make any changes necessary.

e When you are happy that your model works properly, save your work.

f Delete the test data and rename the worksheet Week 1. Create three more worksheets and name them Week 2, Week 3 and Week 4. Copy the model from Week 1 onto each of these worksheets.

g On the Week 1 worksheet, enter the real data for Week 1, which you will find on the New Group Totals tab in the 'Changes' file. Remember to use **Fill Down**, **Fill Right** and **Copy** and **Paste**.

h In the same way, enter the data for Weeks 2–4 on the worksheets for those weeks.

i Save your work.

Task 3

How can you organise the views of these two spreadsheet files to speed up the way you can transfer data:

● yours
● **Resource 4.4 Changes?**

▶ Skills help

Viewing multiple Excel spreadsheets, page 103.

Task 4

You are to prepare a report for the sponsors about the best performances of groups in different weeks. The sponsors want to know:

● days when people did not do much
● days when they all performed well.

1 What is the best way to present this information?

2 How can you use the model to find out who has performed the best?

3 List some ideas for the report before next lesson.

Unit 4.5

In this unit you will create a report containing data from a spreadsheet.

Presenting data from a spreadsheet

Different methods of presentation

Spreadsheets are tables of data. Whole or parts of spreadsheets can be copied as tables into other documents. Here is some data presented in a table.

Item	Price		Takings Week 1	Week 2	Week 3	Week 4	Total
Candy floss	£	2.99	1,286	993	1,429	1,283	4,990
Hot dogs	£	3.25	2,233	2,044	1,615	2,272	8,164
Ice cream tubs	£	1.70	593	546	782	573	2,494
Ice lollies	£	1.00	597	578	704	584	2,463
Bottled water	£	1.50	1,311	1,245	1,473	1,296	5,325
Cans	£	1.50	1,352	1,311	1,460	1,331	5,453
Coffee	£	1.45	365	377	341	355	1,438
Tea	£	1.20	160	144	136	166	605
Total			7,896	7,238	7,939	7,859	30,932

It is not always very easy to identify the important facts coming out of a spreadsheet model just by looking at the tables. If data cannot be easily understood, then different ways of presenting it have to be found. The most common ways are using graphs and charts.

Different types of graph and chart suit different **purposes**. For example, the purpose might be to:

- Compare sales of a range of different products – a **bar chart** is often used for this.

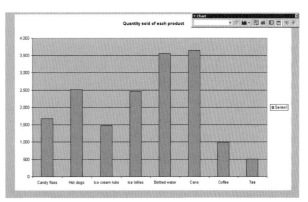

- Look at sales figures over a period of time – **line graphs** are good at showing trends up and down.

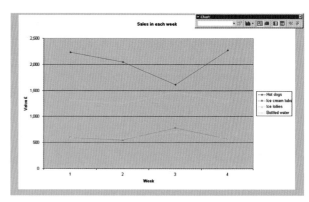

- Show how a budget was split between different items – the important thing here is what proportion of the whole was spent on each thing; a **pie chart** can make this very clear.

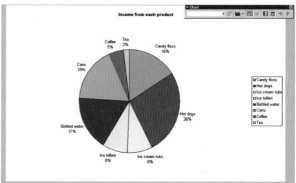

Saving charts and graphs in a spreadsheet

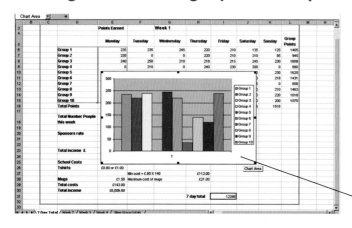

Charts and graphs can be saved either within the spreadsheets on which they are based, or as separate items. If they are saved in the spreadsheet, they can be moved around so they do not cover any of the other information.

Chart saved in worksheet

If they are saved as separate items, a new worksheet is created for each one.

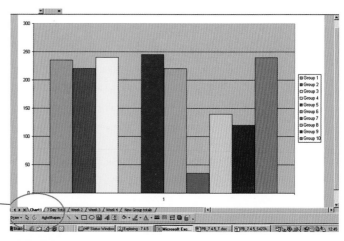

Chart saved as new worksheet

Task 1

 Look at **Resource 4.5 Charts**.

1 Which of these charts do you think is the most effective way to show sponsors the highest scoring group in Week 2?

2 Why do you think it is the clearest?

3 Which format would you choose to show the percentage of points scored by each group?

4 Make notes about the appearance of the different graphs, in preparation to create your own.

Task 2

Open the latest version of your Sponsor Model file.

1 Select the Week 1 tab and create a column chart that shows the total number of points scored each day.

2 Save the chart on a separate worksheet. Rename the tab Week 1 Chart.

3 Do the same for Week 2 but this time create a line graph. Rename this tab Week 2 Graph.

4 Repeat for Week 3 but this time as a pie chart. Rename this tab Week 3 Chart.

5 Which type of chart/graph do you think is the best way to present this data?

6 Select the most effective method and create a chart or graph for Week 4, saving it inside the Week 4 worksheet.

7 Save your work.

Summarising the outcomes of a model for an audience

Sometimes the results or outcomes of your model need to be presented to someone else in the form of a report. You need to think about:

- which bits of information they need?
- what explanatory text you need to add to make it easy for them to understand?
- what form the information should be presented in – tables, charts or graphs?

 Skills help

Creating graphs and charts in Excel, pages 108–9.

Tables, charts and graphs can be placed into documents by using **Copy** and **Paste**. To do this you need to have both the word processing and the spreadsheet programs open. Selected areas are then copied and pasted between the two files.

You can also copy and paste tables, graphs and charts into presentation software in the same way, if you need to present your findings as a slide show instead of a report.

 Skills help

Copying Excel data, graphs and charts into a word processor, page 110.

Using presentation skills in Word, pages 107–8.

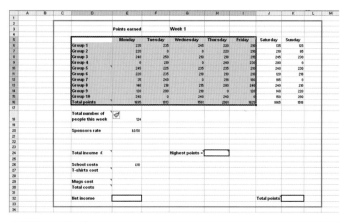

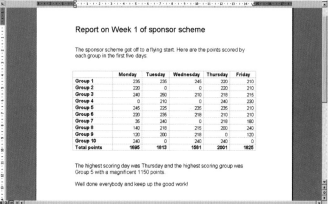

Module Task

It has been decided to produce a weekly bulletin about how the Sponsor Scheme is progressing. It is to be posted on the school notice board. You are going to produce the bulletin for Week 2. It should be no more than 2 sides of A4, and should contain the following information:

- the total number of points scored for the week
- the total amount of money made for the week
- a table showing the points scored by each group on each day of the week
- a chart comparing groups' points performance
- a graph showing the number of points scored on each day of the week
- a chart showing what proportion of the total income actually went to charity, after all costs were taken into account.

a Open a new document in Word and call it 'Bulletin'. Now open the latest version of your Sponsor Model file as well.

b Create the charts and graphs that are needed from your Sponsor Model file. Save them all within the Week 2 worksheet.

c Copy and paste the tables, charts and graphs into place in your 'Bulletin' file. Add any notes you think will be interesting. For example, you might want to give a special mention to the highest scoring group of the week.

d Print off your work.

e Discuss your version of the bulletin with a partner. Do they look the same?

f Make any revisions that you want to.

g Save your work.

Task 3

The sponsors visit the school and see your weekly bulletin. They are particularly interested in the chart showing the proportion of sponsor money which goes to charity. They ask you for a report that shows the difference there would be in one week if the school stopped giving out mugs.

1 Carry out a re-calculation in Week 1 of the Sponsor Scheme without mugs.

2 Produce a chart that can be placed next to one you have already created, to show the effect of stopping giving out mugs.

3 Paste the two graphs into a new document. Add any comments you want.

4 Save your work.

Task 4

You have now carried out a full modelling process.

1 Write a list of three advantages of using a spreadsheet model compared to having to work in other ways.

2 Was it really quicker and easier? If you think so, state how. Could you have done all the same things without using a spreadsheet?

Community playground

To complete Module 4 you are going to set up a model to help Jessie and her friends with a community project that they are involved with.

Background

A group of local residents are looking at creating a local playground facility. The community has raised £10,000 so far and has a sponsor who will give them up to £7500.

They have found out that the most popular pieces of play equipment are:

swings – two types child and toddler

seesaw

trampoline

climbing frame with rope ladders and a scramble net

monkey bars

play tower

slide.

Brief

Set up a model to record the cost for setting up the playground to find out if they can go ahead and purchase all of the equipment that they want.

Work out if they need to raise more money or change their order for equipment.

They have heard that they can get a ten percent discount if they place an order for over £7000.

Work out what is the minimum range of equipment they can buy to get the discount and produce a simple report for the community group containing graphs or charts showing the effect of changing the equipment order.

The cost for each single item is:

Swing child	Swing toddler	Seesaw	Trampoline	Play centre climbing frame	Monkey bars	Play tower	Slide
£95	£99	£120	£325	£800	£85	£1770	£140

To start with they have worked out that they would like to have:

5 child swings	2 play centres with climbing frames
3 toddler swings	2 monkey bars
2 seesaws	1 play tower
2 trampolines	2 slides

There is an added cost for the surface of the playground of £19,000.

The following notes all refer to MS Excel 2000. If you are using a different version, some of the screens may look slightly different, but they should contain similar options.

Software skills

Saving a spreadsheet with a new file name (or for the first time)

1 Click on **File**, **Save** or on the **Save** icon on the main Toolbar. The **Save As** dialogue box opens.

2 Click on the down arrow in the **Save in** window and click on the directory where you want to save your work. You may need to use the up arrow icon to move up the directory tree, or double click on directory names to see the sub directories.

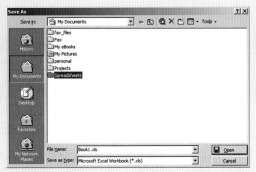

3 Click in the **File name** window and type in a name for your file.

4 Click on **Save**.

Viewing more than one spreadsheet at a time

If you need to copy and paste data from one spreadsheet into another, it is sometimes useful to split the screen and have both spreadsheets visible at the same time.

1 Open both spreadsheets.
2 Click on **Window**, **Arrange**.

3 Click on the **Tiled** button to have the windows side by side.

4 To move between the spreadsheets click on the one you want to be in.

Copying an entire worksheet

1 Click on the grey square at the very top left-hand corner of the worksheet. The whole worksheet should become highlighted.

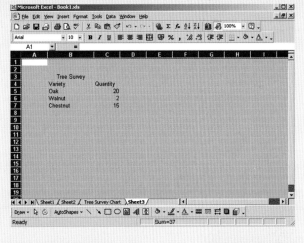

2 Click **Edit**, **Copy**.

3 Click anywhere in the worksheet to remove the highlighting.

4 Click on the tab of the worksheet where you want to paste the original worksheet.

5 Click on the grey square at the top left hand of the worksheet.

6 Click on **Edit**, **Paste**.

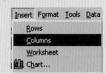

7 Click anywhere in the worksheet to remove the highlighting.

Adding a new worksheet

1 Click on **Insert**, **Worksheet** on the **Menu** bar.

2 A new worksheet will appear.

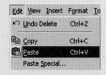

Renaming a worksheet

1 Double-click on the name of the worksheet tab at the bottom right hand of the screen.

2 Type the new name.

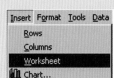

Changing the column width

1 Go to the grey bar at the very top of your worksheet.

2 Click on the small line between the letters at the point where you want to change the column width. The pointer changes to a double arrow symbol.

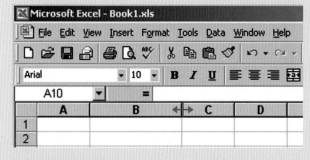

3 Hold down the mouse and drag until the column is the width you want.

4 Click away.

Inserting a row

1 Click in the row below where you would like a new row to appear.

2 Click **Insert**, **Rows**.

Inserting a column

1 Click in the column to the right of where you would like a new column to appear.

2 Click **Insert**, **Columns**.

Deleting a row or column

1 Click on the grey number or letter cell of the row or column you want to delete. The whole row or column should become highlighted.

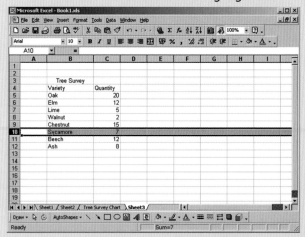

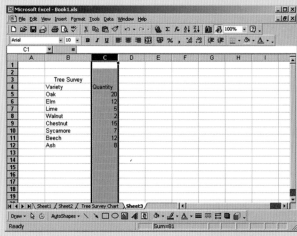

2 Click **Edit**, **Delete**.

Entering data

1 Click on a cell to begin typing.
2 Use the tab key to move one cell to the right.
3 Use the return key to move one cell down.
4 Or you can use the up, down and side arrows or the mouse to move around the spreadsheet.

Changing the font appearance

1 Click in the cells you want to change
2 Click on **Format**, **Cells**. The Format Cells dialogue box opens.

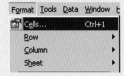

3 Click on the **Font** tab.

4 Scroll down and choose the options you want in the following windows:
   Font
   Font style
   Size
   Underline
   Colour
5 Click to choose any **Effects** such as strikethrough.
6 Click on **OK**.

Quick formatting of font style and size
7 Click in the cells you want to change.
8 To change font style, click the down arrow in the **Font** window on the Formatting toolbar and choose the font you want.

9 To change the font size, click the down arrow in the **Font size** window on the Formatting toolbar and choose the size you want.

Adding backgrounds and borders

1 Click in the cells you want to change.
2 Click on **Format**, **Cells**. The Format Cells dialogue box opens.

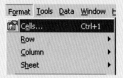

To add borders
3 Click on the **Border** tab.

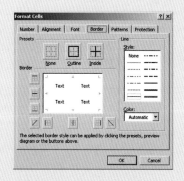

4 Either choose from one of the preset options or click on the diagram to choose where you want your borders to go.
5 Select the **Border Style** from the list on the right.
6 Click on the down arrow in the colour window and choose a colour.
7 Click on **OK**.

To add background colours and patterns
8 Click on the **Patterns** tab.

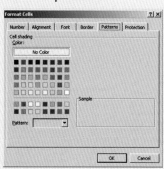

9 Click on the colour you want.
10 Click on the down arrow on the **Pattern** window and choose a pattern if you want to.
11 Click on **OK**.

Formatting numbers

1 Click on the cells you wish to format.

2 Click **Format**, **Cells**. The Format Cells dialogue box appears.

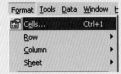

3 Click on the **Number** tab.

4 Scroll down to choose the format you want. Here are some common ones:

Number – choose how many decimal places and whether to have a comma separator for numbers over 1,000.

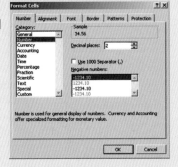

Currency – choose how many decimal places and whether to have the £ symbol.

Date – choose from the list of date formats such as 01/06/03 or 1 June 2003, or 1-Jun.

Percentage – choose how many decimal places.

Copying and pasting cell contents

1 Highlight the cells you want to copy.

2 Click on **Edit**, **Copy**.

3 Click on the top left-hand cell of the ones where you want to paste the data.

4 Click on **Edit**, **Paste**.

Paste special

If you copy and paste a formula you need to think about how you want it to appear when you paste it. If you just click **Edit**, **Paste** the formula itself will be pasted. Sometimes you may want the answer rather than the formula to be pasted. To do this:

1 Click on **Edit**, **Paste Special**.

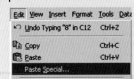

2 Click on the **Values** button.

3 Click on **OK**.

Copying cell contents using the fill handle

1 Click on the cell containing the formula or values that you want to copy.

2 Click on the fill handle at the bottom right-hand corner of the cell, hold and drag until you have covered all the cells you want to fill. Release the mouse button.

NB: you can fill up, down, right or left, always by dragging the fill handle at the bottom right of the cell.

Entering sequences using the fill handle

You can automatically fill cells with data that is in a sequence such as days of the week, months of the year, numbers in sequence, by using the fill handles.

1 Enter the first couple of entries into two adjacent cells.
2 Highlight *both* the cells.
3 Click on the fill handle and drag until you have covered as many cells as you want filled with the sequence. Release the mouse button and you will get the sequence of numbers appearing in the cells.

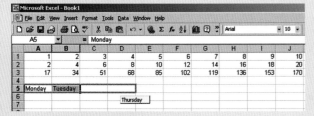

Formula skills

Adding up a list of numbers

1 To add up a list of numbers you can either write each one out:
=B5+B4+B5+B6
2 or you can instruct the computer to find the Sum of a range of numbers:
=SUM(B5:B10)

Auto sum

1 Highlight the list of numbers you want to add up, plus a blank cell.
2 Click on the **Auto Sum** button on the main toolbar. Σ
The =SUM formula is automatically entered and the result calculated.

Relative cell referencing

If you copy a formula using either copy and paste or the fill handle, the software will automatically adjust the cell references within the formula to the new position.

| =D15+E15+F15+G15+H15+H15 |
| =D16+E16+F16+G16+H16+H16 |

Absolute cell referencing

Sometimes we do not want the computer to adjust the cell references when we copy a formula. The way to stop it is to type $ in front of *both bits* of the cell reference, i.e. in front of the letter *and* the number: e.g. **$B$2**.

| =D15+E15+F15+G15+$H$15 |
| =D16+E16+F16+G16+$H$15 |

Absolute cell referencing is useful if you have one particular piece of fixed information, for example a price, which you want to keep referring to in lots of different formulas.

Presentation skills

Creating a chart/graph

1 Highlight the cells containing the data, including labels, which you want to appear in the chart.
2 Click on **Insert**, **Chart**. The Chart Wizard opens with the Step 1 dialogue box.
3 Scroll down the **Chart Type** window and choose the type of chart or graph you want.

4 Click on the right-hand side to select any **Chart sub-type** you want to choose.
5 Click **Next**. Step 2 dialogue box appears.
6 Click **Next**. Step 3 dialogue box appears.
7 Type a title for your chart in the **Chart title** window.

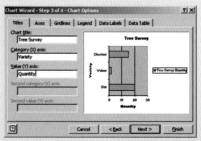

8 Type a label for the horizontal (X) axis in the **Category (X) axis** window.

9 Type a label for the vertical (Y) axis in the **Value (Y) axis** window.

10 Click on the **Legend** tab.

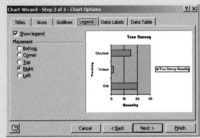

11 Click to select the legend and choose a **Placement** position, or click again to remove the legend.

12 Click on the **Data Labels** tab.

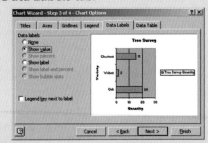

13 Click on buttons to choose whether to show value, percent, label, etc.

14 Click **Next**. Step 4 dialogue box appears.

15 Click on buttons to choose where to place your chart.

- To place it in a new worksheet, click on **As new sheet** and type a name for the worksheet in the window.
- To place it within an existing worksheet, click on **As object in**. Click the down arrow on the window to select which worksheet you want to place it in. You can click anywhere on the chart/graph and drag it to where you want it to appear.

16 Click on **Finish**.

NB: Depending on which type of graph or chart you choose, not all of these steps may be necessary. For example, pie charts do not require X and Y axis labels.

Creating a chart or graph from non-adjacent columns

1 Click and drag the data (column labels, row labels and data) in the first column required.

2 Hold down the control (Ctrl) key and click and drag the data (column labels, row labels and data) from the next required column.

Gender	Height (cm)	Foot length (cm)	Mobile phone	Computer
M	149	19	No	Yes
F	155	21	Yes	Yes
F	133	21	No	Yes
F	160	26	Yes	Yes
M	143	24	No	Yes
F	146	23	Yes	No
M	150	22	No	Yes

3 You can keep on adding columns by holding down the control key (Ctrl) until all the required data is selected. Then follow instructions for creating a chart.

Word processing skills

Here are some useful skills to help you to produce a professional-looking report in Word.

Page numbering

1 Click on **Insert**, **Page Numbers**. The **Page Numbers** dialogue box appears.

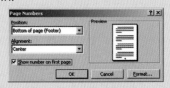

2 Click on the down arrow in the **Position** window and choose the position you want the numbers to appear in.

3 Click on the down arrow on the **Alignment** window to choose the alignment.

4 Make sure the **Show number on first page box** is ticked.

5 Click on **Format**. The **Page Number Format** dialogue box appears.

6 Click on the down arrow on the **Number format** window and choose the format you want.

7 Click on **OK** twice.

Inserting bullet points or numbered lists

1 Either click where you want a new list to appear, or highlight some existing text that you want to format as bullets or a list.

2 Click on **Format**, **Bullets and Numbering**. The Bullets and Numbering dialogue box appears.

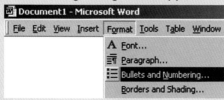

To insert bullet points

3 Click on the Bulleted tab.

4 Click to select the kind of bullets you want.

5 Click on **OK**.

To insert a numbered list

6 Click on the Numbered tab.

7 Click to select the number format you want.

8 Click on **OK**.

Special note: you can also use the icons on the formatting toolbar to create bullets and numbered lists:

9 Highlight the text as before.

10 Click on the Numbering icon or the Bullet points icon.

Wrapping text around pictures

If you import graphs or charts or tables into your document, it can sometimes look better if you wrap the text around the pictures, as in the example below.

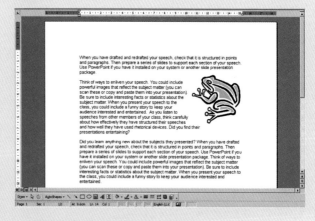

1 Click on the object that you want to wrap the text around, such as a picture or graph.

2 Click **Format**, **Picture**. The **Format Picture** dialogue box appears.

3 Click on the **Layout** tab.

4 Click to select the layout you prefer. Square is probably the most useful.

5 Click on **OK**.

You can now either type around the picture or move the picture into place and the text will automatically wrap around it.

Integrating software skills

Copy spreadsheet data for use in a word processor

1 Highlight the data in your spreadsheet which you would like to copy.

Business visits	Holiday visits	Miscellaneous
18.15%	46.46%	18.05%
19.18%	44.28%	18.48%
20.65%	44.11%	16.57%
21.42%	43.98%	14.63%
20.57%	45.25%	13.48%
20.51%	46.68%	12.28%
20.98%	46.80%	12.97%
20.86%	46.13%	13.08%
23.65%	42.59%	12.56%
22.89%	43.86%	12.82%

2 Click on **Edit**, **Copy**.

3 Switch to the word processor.

4 Click in the place you want the data to be displayed.

5 Click **Edit**, **Paste**.

Business visits	Holiday visits	Miscellaneous
18.15%	46.46%	18.05%
19.18%	44.28%	18.48%
20.65%	44.11%	16.57%
21.42%	43.98%	14.63%
20.57%	45.25%	13.48%
20.51%	46.68%	12.28%
20.98%	46.80%	12.97%
20.86%	46.13%	13.08%
23.65%	42.59%	12.56%
22.89%	43.86%	12.82%

Special Note: This pastes a table containing the data. The table can be formatted to change the way the data is displayed. Using this method does NOT link data, so any changes made in the spreadsheet are not reflected in the word processor.

Linking data between spreadsheet and word processor

1 Highlight the data to be inserted as before.

2 Click on **Edit**, **Copy**.

3 Switch to the word processor.

4 Click in the place you want the data to be displayed.

5 Click **Edit**, **Paste Special**. The **Paste Special** dialogue box opens.

6 Click on **Paste link**.

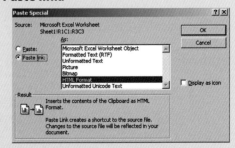

This will maintain a link between the data file and the document.

Copy a spreadsheet graph for use in a word processor

1 In your spreadsheet, click on the graph you would like to copy.

2 Click **Edit**, **Copy**.

3 Switch to the word processor.

4 Click in the place you want the graph to be displayed.

5 Click on **Edit**, **Paste**.

In this module you will create a data handling file and enter some data in it. You will learn how to use the software to search for information and answer questions.

Before you start, there are some skills and words that you will need to know. Read about each skill in the boxes below and then decide which of the following statements best describes how you feel about it:

A I am confident that I understand / can do this.
B I think I understand / can do this, but I would like to check.
C I definitely don't know how to do this and I need to learn.

Understanding the structure of a simple database

A **database** consists of many **records**. Each record has several **fields** each containing one piece of data. The fields on each record in a database are always exactly the same.

Record All the information about one particular person or product in a database e.g. name, gender, age, etc.

Field One single piece of information in a database e.g. surname.

When you look at a whole database it looks like a table or spreadsheet. The fields are the columns and the rows are the records.

	A	B	C	D	E
1	**Record Number**	**First name**	**Surname**	**Gender**	**Age**
2	1	Stephen	Jones	M	14
3	2	Anna	Karenina	F	16
4	3	James	Phillips	M	13
5	4	Harry	Potter	M	13
6	5	Mandy	Smith	F	14
7	6	John	Wilman	M	12

Entering data into a database

Data is entered by typing in the data or in some databases the data is transferred automatically. The data is entered in different **data types**.

Data types. Different data types are used so that calculations, searches and sorts on data can be done efficiently. The two main types of data are **alphanumeric** and **numeric**.

Mr S. Claus,
1. North Pole Street,
LAPLAND.
AR6 2LP

Alphanumeric data. This can be a mixture of numbers and text. A postcode is alphanumeric.

Numeric data. This is limited to numbers only. The numbers can be formatted in different ways, for example as a percentage, a date or a currency.

Carrying out simple queries using a database

In order to find a specific piece of information from a database, it is necessary to carry out a **query**.

Query A query is a question which is asked to a computer. For example, 'find me all the girls whose first name begins with S.' The data in a database can be sorted and searched in order to find the answer to the query.

Sorted The data is put in order either alphabetically or numerically.

Searched The software looks for all the records which match the criteria in the query. Some database software does this by filtering.

Filtering Allows you to see just the data you want – it filters out unwanted data.

Conducting a questionnaire

Questionnaires are used to collect data that is entered into data files. The questions in a questionnaire are used to help to test out a **hypothesis**.

Hypothesis. This is an idea that can be tested by finding evidence from the data in a database. For example, 'Girls get more pocket money than boys' is a hypothesis.

Creating reports from a database

The data from a database can be used to create **reports** which may include text, tables and graphs and charts. Reports may be exported into other packages such as Word processing or presentation software.

Report A summary of information which has been found by running one or more queries on the data in a database.

Task

 Look at **Resource 5 Circus acts**.

1. Write down the names of all the fields in the first record.

2. Write down the names of all the acts which involve animals.

3. Which act has the most performers?

4. Are there more acts needing safety nets than not?

5. Create a bar chart to show the popularity rating of the acts. Print it out.

Unit 5.1
Looking at data

In this unit you will look at some information from a database. You will consider the reliability of the data and learn that charts and graphs can help you understand the data.

What is a database?

A **database** is a collection of data that has been structured in a useful way and stored in a computer. It acts as an information source and allows the user to retrieve the information in a variety of different ways. Some databases are very large.

A database is used to search and sort data that would be difficult to search through by hand.

For example, imagine you had to find everyone in the school whose name begins with the letter P who is male, or all 14-year-old students whose surnames begin with J. What a nightmare! How long would that take to go through all student records by hand?

'I know it's in here somewhere'

Classified information

The data which is held in each record of a database can be used to **classify** that record. To classify means to put into groups according to certain **criteria**. For example, all people can be classified as either male or female.

Here are two classifications:

Gender   Age

If these two pieces of data are held for each person in the school database then the computer could easily find only the records in which the Gender field contains the word Male or the Age field contains the number 14. Because the data is organised into fields, it is also easy to tell the computer to find only the records which have the Surname field beginning with J or the First name field beginning with P.

Types of database

A **flat file** database is a simple database. All the data is stored in one table, just like a spreadsheet. In this module you will be using flat file databases. The examples you will look at have been created in MS Excel, which can be used to create simple databases as well as spreadsheets

A flat file database is easy to set up and provides a good way to search, sort and filter data. For carrying out more complicated searches and sorts the data needs to be stored in a **relational database**. A relational database is made up of a number of linked tables. An example of software which can create a relational database is MS Access. You will probably move on to using a relational database later in the course.

In the rest of this unit you will be looking at data which has been extracted from large databases and learning how to use it to find out information. The data is held in Excel tables and you will be developing some of the skills which you learned in Module 4.

Task 1

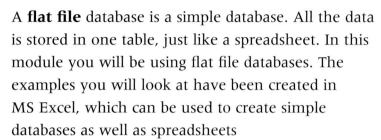

Look at **Resource 5.1 Numbers**.

1 This shows a lot of **numerical** data. What do the numbers represent?

2 Are all the numbers presented in the same format?

3 What does <15 and 65+ mean on this table?

4 What are the general things you could find out from this data?

Module Task

Look at **Resource 5.1 Numbers**.

Work with a partner to answer these questions about information in the data file.

1 In which countries can men expect to live to over 75?

2 Which country had the highest population in mid-2002?

3 Which countries have more 65+ year-olds than <15-year-olds.

4 Which country has the highest population per square mile?

Now look at **Resource 5.1 Population**. Try questions 1–4 again. How did the software make it easier for you to find the answers? Complete the following questions using **Resource 5.1 Population**.

5 Most people live in urban areas in the United Kingdom. Is this true? Which country has the fewest people living in an urban area?

6 The **origin** of this data is an American website. The **URL** for the website can be accessed via http://www.heinemann.co.uk/hotlinks. Is this an official website? Is the data **reliable**?

How reliable is the data?

It is always a good idea to check the source of your data. Questions you should ask are:

Is it an official source?	You should always check and make a note of the name of the website or other source where you got the data
Is it up to date?	Many official websites do not keep their data up to date!
Is it incomplete?	The data may show only part of the picture you are investigating
Is it likely to be biased?	For example, was the data produced by a company that has an interest in putting a certain point of view?
How big is the sample?	If you are investigating something nationally, you would get a distorted picture if you only looked at data from one locality.

Graphs and charts

Graphs and charts are an effective way to display data from a database so that it can be easily understood. There is a range of different types of chart that can be used to show different types of data.

A **column chart** is useful for comparing data.

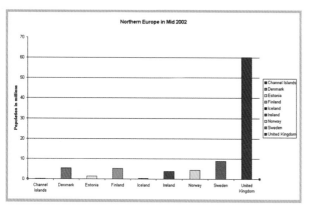

A **line graph** is good for showing **trends** and looking at growth rates.

If you have already done Module 4, you will have learned about how to produce graphs and charts in Excel. These skills will be useful in the first two units of Module 5.

Task 2

 Look at **Resource 5.1 Population**.

Find the answers to these questions.
- *What is the trend for the population in Italy? Does it increase or decrease?*
- *Why do you think the population per square mile for the Channel Islands and Malta is high?*

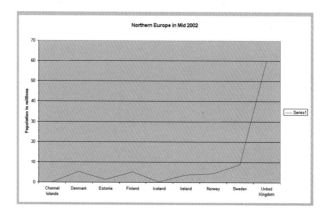

Task 3

 Look at **Resource 5.1 Population**.

1 Create a column chart to show population in mid-2002 to cover the countries from the Channel Islands to the United Kingdom. Place it in the Population worksheet.

2 Use the same data to make a line graph, also in the Population worksheet. Which is easier to read?

3 Save the file with a new file name in the shared area.

 Skills help

Creating graphs and charts in Excel, pages 107–8.

Task 4

● Before the next lesson, collect three different graphs from newspapers, magazines or from the Internet that show data in a way that is easy to understand.

● Make comments on why you think they are clear.

Unit 5.2
Presenting information

In this unit you will learn how to use data to draw conclusions and to present information in different formats, such as percentages and graphs.

Proposing a hypothesis

A **hypothesis** is a statement made for the purpose of testing its truth. For example: 'the number of packets of crisps sold increases if it is raining'.

You can use data to help you draw conclusions about a hypothesis and test whether it is true or not.

Task 1

1 Write down a hypothesis about students in your class. Perhaps you think that:
   - all boys are taller than girls
   - school bags get heavier as the week goes on
   - you get more homework at the beginning of the week.

2 Discuss your hypothesis with the rest of the class. How could you test it?

'You can tell it's Friday, can't you?'

Testing a hypothesis

To test whether a hypothesis is true you need to have some data which is:
- relevant
- measurable.

So, to test the hypothesis that the number of packets of crisps sold increases if it is raining, you would need data on rainfall and on numbers of packets of crisps sold.

Look at **Resource 5.2 Weather data** and **Resource 5.2 Prove it!**.

1 Think of a hypothesis that you could test from this data.
One hypothesis might be that the rainfall in January increased every year between 1982 and 1997. Another might be that the sunniest months recorded were all in 1992.

2 Work with your partner and record your hypothesis. Make notes on how you think it could be tested.

3 Will a graph or chart help to present the data?

Drawing conclusions from data

Once you have tested your hypothesis, it is important to check that your conclusions are **plausible**.

- Are they what you expected?
- Are they supported by the data?
- Do they prove that your hypothesis was right or wrong?
- Could there be another conclusion which is also supported by the same data – perhaps with a different **viewpoint**?

 Look at **Resource 5.2 Weather data**.

Quite a complex hypothesis could be tested on this data, for example:

- January 1985 was the sunniest and wettest month for 10 years
- a hot spell happens in the summer every three years.

1 Add a second, more complex, hypothesis to your notes, and ask a partner to test it out. Do they think that it is plausible after testing?

YEAR	JAN	FEB	MAR	ANNUAL TOTAL
1982	39.7	25.7	61.8	671.4
1983	90.6	22	60.5	801
1984	99.2	46	43	758.6
1985	50.3	23.8	40.2	624.5
1986	86.7	1.6	62.4	775.6
1987	20	39.3	74.2	805.4
1988	108.8	27.1	110.3	793.7
1989	28.7	56.6	42.1	689.5
1990	86	72.9	11.7	684.4
1991	41.4	36.5	50	480.5
1992	38.7	54.5	66.5	741.1
1993	55.8	5.8	10.6	651.6
1994	50	34.6	60.6	752.1
1995	99.8	71.2	55.2	621.2
1996	13.4	35.2	26.8	591.4
1997	3.8	50.4	21	774.2

YEAR	JAN %	FEB %	MAR %	ANNUAL TOTAL
1982	5.9%	3.8%	9.2%	671.4
1983	11.3%	2.7%	7.6%	801
1984	13.1%	6.1%	5.7%	758.6
1985	8.1%	3.8%	6.4%	624.5
1986	11.2%	0.2%	8.0%	775.6
1987	2.5%	4.9%	9.2%	805.4
1988	13.7%	3.4%	13.9%	793.7
1989	4.2%	8.2%	6.1%	689.5
1990	12.6%	10.7%	1.7%	684.4
1991	8.6%	7.6%	10.4%	480.5
1992	5.2%	7.4%	9.0%	741.1
1993	8.6%	0.9%	1.6%	651.6
1994	6.6%	4.6%	8.1%	752.1
1995	16.1%	11.5%	8.9%	621.2
1996	2.3%	6.0%	4.5%	591.4
1997	0.5%	6.5%	2.7%	774.2

Using percentages to help to understand data

Sometimes it is useful to look at numbers in a table as percentages of the total. This can assist with comparing data. It can also sometimes enable the user to get new information from the data. In the examples opposite, the first table has all of the numerical values written out in full, and the second one has the same data as percentages of the total.

It is much easier to compare how wet it was in the months of a year using the second table.

▶ *Skills help*

Formatting cells in Excel, pages 105–6

Using formulas in Excel, page 107.

Calculating percentages in Excel, page 136.

Module Task

 Look at **Resource 5.2 Weather data**.

This is a data file comparing information on the weather in a number of countries. It will be more useful if presented as percentages.

a Click on the worksheet 'Creating %' on the menu tab at the bottom of the screen.

b Click on cell H4. Look at the formula bar.

   The formula '=B4/E4' works out the January rainfall as a percentage (%) of the total rainfall for the year. The number format of the cell has been set to **Percentage** instead of **Number**.

c Click on the worksheet 'Your turn' on the menu tab at the bottom of the screen.

d Insert the **formulas** which will create percentages from the Sunshine data for Jan, Feb and Mar of each year. The number format of the cells has already been set to **Percentage**. Remember you can copy formulas.

e Save your work and print it out.

Collecting data

The data that has been used in this unit had to be collected (over a long period of time). Sometimes the data we need in order to test a hypothesis does not exist and we need to collect it. One way of doing this is to ask people questions and record their answers in a table.

Task 4

Before the next lesson you are to collect some data from a range of different people about holidays.

 Look at **Resource 5.2 Collection**.

This is an example of how to record data on a table – use it to help you when answering the questions below.

1 Here are some questions for you to ask:
   a Where do you go on holiday?
   b Where would you visit for a day out?
   c Did your parents go to the same places when they were your age?
   d Did your grandparents?

2 Collect the data from four different people:
   - a person who is younger than you
   - a friend
   - one of your parents or someone their age
   - one of your grandparents or someone their age.

3 Record the data you collect from your interviews in a table.

Unit 5.3
Creating a questionnaire

In this unit you will design a questionnaire which will collect relevant data in a suitable format so that you can test a hypothesis.

Questionnaires and the right response

In Module 2 you started to work with **surveys** and **questionnaires**. In this unit you are going to build on your understanding of how to set up questionnaires. You will study how to set questions in a way that gets an answer in the format that you want.

 Make sure the questions in your questionnaire are relevant to your hypothesis.

Task 1

In Unit 5.2 you collected data about holidays and days out from interviews with your family and friends.

1 Working with a partner, look at the sets of data you both have collected.

2 Write down a hypothesis to test, based upon the data that the two of you have collected. For example, one hypothesis might be: 'None of our grandparents ever had holidays abroad when they were young'.

3 Talk to other students to test out your hypothesis and see whether it is true by looking at as many sets of their data as possible.

4 Now you have seen more sets of data, work out a series of ten questions that could be asked nationally (through a questionnaire) to try to test out your hypothesis. For example:
- *How many holidays did you take?*
- *Did you go with your parents?*
- *Did you fly, go by boat, car, bus or train?*

What data is required?

When writing a questionnaire in order to collect data to test a hypothesis, you must think very carefully about the **type of data** that is required. For example, if the hypothesis is 'Boys are taller than girls', you would need to collect data on height and sex.

What else might you need to know? Remember you are going to be making comparisons. If you compared a 5-year-old boy and a 15-year-old girl would that enable you to draw any plausible conclusions?

What questions do I need to ask to get that data?

Once you know exactly the data you need, the next step is to write questions which will get that data. Not all questions are as simple as the ones in the example above.

What type of answers do I want?

Module 2 covers in detail the different types of questions used in questionnaires and the type of answers you might get. Here are some of them:

- descriptive responses (free text)
- yes or no answers (Yes or No)
- a numerical range (0 is low and 5 is high)
- a text range (poor is low and excellent is high).

In order to test a hypothesis, the data which is collected must be sorted and classified (put into groups) using a computer. The answers which you put into your database need to be very precise. For this reason, it is a good idea to make all or most of the questions on a questionnaire 'closed' questions, with only a limited range of possible answers.

Task 2

 Look at **Resource 5.3 Questionnaire**

You are going to use your ideas so far to help you to test the hypothesis:

> **12-year-olds have more foreign holidays today than they would have had in the 1970s.**

1 *Plan your questions and put them in a table with a column headed 'Questions'.*

2 *Put answers that you might get into an 'Answers' column.*

3 *Are all of the questions to do with the subject? For example, would it matter which months the holidays were in?*

 ## Skills help

Setting questions for questionnaires, page 47.

Task 3

1 *Open the Questions and Answers table you made in Task 2.*

2 *For each question and answer, think about how easy it would be for a computer to sort and classify the data.*

3 *Suggest ways in which the questions and answers could be improved.*

Module Task

a You are to create a questionnaire, or data collection form, based on the questions and answers developed in Tasks 2 and 3. You can use either word processing or spreadsheet software for this.

Check that your questions will let you find out:
- *Name* First name, second name, and so on.
- *Age* This is an important piece of data.
- *How many holidays they had* A range of numbers.
- *How many foreign holidays they had* A range of numbers.

Remember the data you get has to be processed by a computer.

b Save your work in the shared area.

c Print off your questionnaire.

 Skills help

Editing and formatting text in Excel, page 105.

Who should you ask?

Another key factor to consider is who the questionnaire will be answered by. There can be quite a difference between data collected from the whole country on a national level and that collected at a local level.

National data includes data from rural areas and the middle of large cities, so a wide viewpoint is covered. Local data comes from within a small area, for example the community that lives around a school, so it shows the viewpoint of the area.

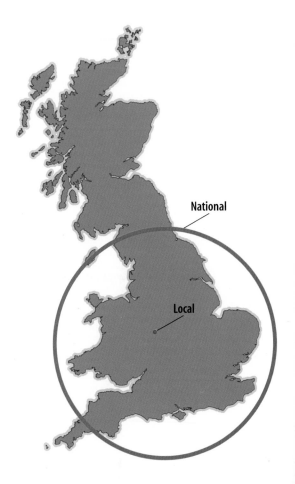

National

Local

Case study

Employment data was collected in two very different localities, and in each case the local data was compared with national data. The two column charts below show how the local data varies greatly between the two localities.

In each pair of columns the national data (which is the same in both graphs) is on the left, and the local data is on the right.

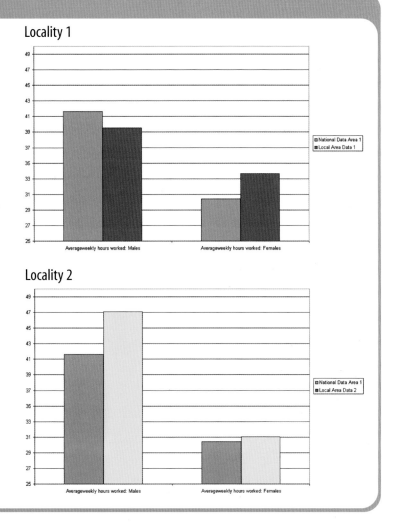

Locality 1

Locality 2

Questions used for collecting data should be phrased in such a way that they can be answered by anyone, wherever they live.

National data is often collected through postal questionnaires, whereas local data can be collected through interviews. Usually surveys involve both types of data collection.

Task 4

Use the questionnaire you created in the Module Task to collect some local sample data.

1 *Who are you going to ask? (Remember the hypothesis you want to test.)*
   ● *someone younger than you?*
   ● *a friend?*
   ● *your parents or someone their age?*
   ● *your grandparents or someone their age?*

2 *Ask your **sample** group of people for their responses. Bring the completed questionnaires to the next lesson.*

Unit 5.4
Creating a data handling file

In this unit you will learn to refine your methods of questioning and design a data handling file that will enable you to test a hypothesis.

Refining a questionnaire

The questions that make up a questionnaire should all help to build a set of data that will test whether a hypothesis is true or not. The responses to your questions should contain data which will enable you to separate or classify then into groups. Look back at Unit 5.1 if you need reminding about classifying data.

Hypothesis:
People watch TV for more than 5 hours each day

In order to test this hypothesis, you must be able to separate or classify the respondents into two groups which can be counted:

Group 1: all the people who watch TV for more than 5 hours a day

Group 2: all those who watch TV for less than 5 hours a day (which could include not watching it at all!).

Here's how you could do this using a questionnaire.
Question 1: Do you watch TV each day?
Answer: Yes or No

If they answer 'No', then they do not need to answer any more questions, but you must record that they have answered 'No', as this is important in testing the hypothesis.

If they answer 'Yes', you could ask them:
Question 2: How many hours do you watch TV each day?
Answer: 1 2 3 4 5 6 7 8 9 more

But in order to test the hypothesis, the only thing you need to know is if they watch more than 5 hours or not, so you could refine Question 2 by restricting the answers to:
1–4 hours   5 or more hours

Results: All those who answered 'No' and all those who answered '1–4 hours' go into one classification, and all those who answered '5 hours or more' go into the other classification. The totals in each group will tell you whether the hypothesis is true or not.

'Well, my Gran says that life is just one big holiday these days!'

Task 1

You have been doing some work on the hypothesis:

12-year-olds have more foreign holidays today than they would have had in the 1970s.

You worked on a set of questions and asked a sample of people for their answers. Using the TV example on page 126 to help you, work with your partner to refine your questionnaire. You might want to combine to produce one between you. Think about:

1 Are the answers you received any help to test out the hypothesis?

2 Could they be classified?

3 Do all the questions need to be answered by all age groups?

4 Check that your questions are:
   - precise
   - easy to answer
   - only give one answer
   - in a form that you can sort (classify) into groups
   - in a sensible order.

5 Agree a final set of questions and possible answers with your partner first and then with the rest of the class.

Creating a data handling file

In order to sort and classify the responses to a questionnaire, they need to be put into a database which will have the following functions:

- It will allow data to be entered quickly, easily and accurately
- It will allow data to be sorted and classified in order to test a hypothesis.

To make data-entry as easy as possible, each field in a data handling file should be formatted according to the **data type** (**text**, **alphanumeric** or **numeric**) which will be in it.

Wherever possible, data should be abbreviated when it is input. So, for example, instead of Yes or No, you could type Y or N into the data handling file.

Questionnaires need to be short and to the point. People do not want to answer lots of questions when one would do the same job.

Task 2

Change the hypothesis from Task 1 to:

12-year-olds have more and longer foreign holidays today than they would have had in the 1970s.

1 What does this do to the way the questions are put together?

2 Write a set of questions that can be used to test this hypothesis.

Data types
Text and alphanumeric data should always be formatted as text. Only format cells as numbers if you want to perform calculations on the data.

Module Task

You are to set up a data handling file to enter the data from the class questionnaire that you have refined and agreed in Task 1. It will be a flat file database created in Excel.

a Load Excel and open a new worksheet.

b Decide which questions have the answers that you need to test your hypothesis. Type these question numbers as field names across the top of the worksheet. (Remember not every question will be answered by every respondent.)

c For each question, make a list of all the possible answers in the form you are going to use them in the database (for example Y or N, 1, 2, 3, etc).

d Format the fields (columns) according to whether the answers are text, numeric or alphanumeric.

e Print a copy of your data handling file.

f Save your work in the shared area.

g Your teacher will give you a copy of the final version of the questionnaire, as agreed by the class. Using the data which you gathered in Unit 5.3 Task 4, complete this questionnaire and give it back to your teacher.

 Skills help

Setting up a data structure in Excel, page 136.

Task 3

1 Look at the printed copy of your data handling file from the Module Task.

Think about the design of it in terms of:
- ease of entering the data
- ease of classifying data.

2 Annotate your printout with things that you would like to change.

3 Ask a partner for their evaluation.

Evaluating questionnaires

There are several key factors that should be checked before presenting a questionnaire to the public. Professional researchers always check that their questionnaires have considered:

- the full range of answers to each question on the questionnaire, even *unlikely* ones
- how to classify answers that are outside the range expected
- if space has been made for a range of numeric answers (so that there are no answers outside the expected range)
- the benefit of short answers and abbreviations for common entries, in order to cut down the number of key strokes for entering the data into a computer.

Unit 5.5
Entering, checking and testing data

In this unit you will learn how to enter data and use graphs or charts to check the accuracy of the data. You will also learn how to sort and search data.

Data entry

Many people are employed to input data. Their job is to transfer data that has come into an organisation into database systems. The data can vary and may be anything from product orders to responses to questionnaires. They have to make sure that they can work fast and **efficiently**.

It is important to check that data has been entered correctly and accurately in order to be able to draw conclusions **effectively**. A data handling program cannot tell whether the data is sensible or correct.

Data entry clerks processing customer orders.

Types of error

The most common errors are:

- data entered incorrectly, for example spelling mistakes – can be checked automatically with software
- wrong data type, for example text when numerical data is expected – can be checked automatically
- missing entries, where data was not collected – needs to be looked for manually as a 'no entry' may be correct
- wrong key used, for example the single key 'Y' (for yes) may be pressed instead of 'N' (for no) – can only be found manually by reading the file against the original data.

Finding errors

There are several methods of checking data and these generally fall into two categories:

- automated methods
- manual methods, such as proofreading.

Proofreading is suitable if there is not too much data, but an automated process is better if large amounts of data are involved. Sometimes it's worth using a combination of both methods.

Automated methods include:

- using a spellchecker
- converting the data into a graph or chart – the mistakes are often much more easy to spot in a graphical mode
- using a validation formula – for example if the answer is a range between 1–5 you can tell the computer to reject any number outside that range
- sorting the data – odd ones out can become more obvious.

 *Look at **Resource 5.5 Trails**.*

Task 1

1 *Can you spot the errors in the data entry?*

2 *How many do you think there are? Check with your partner to see whether you got them all.*

3 *How could these be checked?*

4 *Is there a way that this could be prevented from happening?*

'Are you sure this is what Sajid meant when he said to look closely for mistakes'

Task 2

1 Load the data handling file you created in Unit 5.4.

2 Your teacher will give you the responses to the class questionnaire. Working with your partner, enter the data into your data handling file. Watch out for any entry errors.

3 Can you work out a way that will help speed up the process between you – for example, one types, one reads?

4 Save your work at regular intervals. This means that if anything goes wrong with the data entry you will only lose the data between the fault and the previous 'Save'.

5 Once you have finished capturing your data you can create a column chart to see if there are any obvious errors in the data.

 Look at **Resource 5.5 Errors** to see how graphs can help to show up errors.

Sorting and searching data

Once data entry is complete it is possible to start using it to answer questions. This is done by running **queries**. There are two main types of query which will be used in this module: **Sorting** and **Searching**.

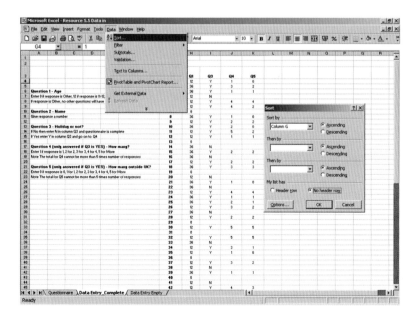

Sorting

When data is sorted, it is displayed in order, either numerically or alphabetically, according to whichever sort fields are chosen. It is possible to sort by two or three different fields at the same time.

Searching

Searching is used to display only entries of a set value, for example all 12-year-olds. In Excel this is done using the Filtering tool.

AND/OR enquiries

You can use combinations of sorts and filters to carry out more complex searches. This may involve doing AND/OR queries.

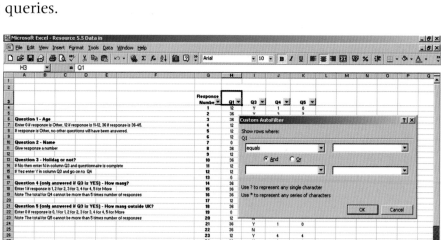

If you filter more than one column at the same time, you are doing an AND enquiry. For example you could filter on Age and on Number of holidays to find all people who are 12 years old AND who had 2 holidays. Only those who fit *both* of those criteria will be shown.

An OR enquiry means you ask the computer to find all people who fit *either* one criteria OR another. For example you could search for all the people who had *either* 3 OR 4 holidays.

Task 3

 Look at **Resource 5.4 Data in**.

1 Use the Sort or Filter options to find out:
- how many people went on holiday twice
- how many people went away three or more times.

2 Use an **AND** search to find out:
- how many 36-45 year olds did not go on holiday?

Skills help

Sorting, filtering and searching data in Excel, page 137.

Module Task

a Open your own data file from Task 2.

b Write down five questions similar to the ones in Tasks 3 and 4. Try to think of questions which would be helpful in testing the hypothesis: **12-year-olds have more foreign holidays today than they would have had in the 1970s.**

c Use Sort and Filter enquiries to answer the questions. When you have performed each enquiry, write down the questionnaire sheet numbers as the answers (or results) to the questions. Remember to reset the data each time before starting the next enquiry.

d Ask your partner to search the database with the same questions. Do they get the same results?

e Write down any additional data you need to improve accuracy.

Task 4

1 Find out the number of 12-year-olds who went on holiday between 2 and 4 times. Write down the questionnaire numbers.

2 How many people only holidayed in their home country? What percentage of these were 36- or 45-year-olds?

3 Check your findings with a partner.

Unit 5.6
Drawing conclusions from data

In this unit you will learn how to draw conclusions from your database. You will select specific data for a report that will contain evidence to support your conclusion.

Conclusions

In the last unit you carried out enquiries on your data to gather **evidence** to test a hypothesis. When you have gathered all the relevant evidence it is time to draw your **conclusions**. This means deciding whether the hypothesis is correct or not, based on the evidence you have found.

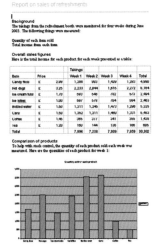

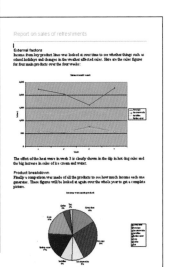

Remember, the evidence may not support your hypothesis! If it does not, that could mean one of two things:

EITHER The hypothesis was wrong.
OR The evidence you have used is wrong.

It does not matter if your hypothesis is proved wrong, so long as you are sure that the evidence you have found is accurate and plausible.

Conclusions or decisions can be presented in a **report**. The report should present the major facts that have been found. It needs clear statements of conclusions supported by evidence.

Evidence can appear as graphs, tables, bullet points, lists, charts. Sometimes it is clearer to present figures as percentages. The more complex the conclusions, the simpler the presentation of the evidence needs to be. These are some formats used for formal reports.

How plausible are your conclusions?

Plausible means believable. Evidence is gathered to check the plausibility of a hypothesis.

Imaginary case

Hypothesis: Half of the population is men.

Response: Well, that sounds plausible. If they aren't men then they are women, so there are just two possibilities: 50% men and 50% women.

Evidence: We need real data to prove the statement and to test that it is really plausible. We don't know that an equal number of male and female babies are born every year. Evidence must be obtained to support the statement.

For data to provide plausible evidence it must be:

Accurate	Has the data been thoroughly checked for errors at inputting stage?
Representative	Is the data drawn from a national survey, or does it represent a local viewpoint? Is the sample sufficiently big to prove the hypothesis?
Reliable	Is the data up-to-date? Is the source a reliable one?

Task 1

 Look at **Resource 5.6 Music.**

1 What do you think of the way the questions are asked?

2 Can you guess the answers to the questions by looking at the way the data is presented?

3 Which is the better method of writing the statements?

4 If you had to write an article for the school newsletter about the choice of music by Key Stage 3 students, can you think of a good way to present the data?

'So you're telling me that 10% of the 15% that know how to sing think that 20% of them are good!'

Module Task

Let's look at our hypothesis:

12-year-olds have more foreign holidays today than they would have had in the 1970s.

a *Could you find evidence in your data to support it?*

b *What other things did you find out about from the data?*

c *Write a list of four conclusions that you can make based on the data.*

*Make it clear that this gives a **viewpoint** from a local area.*

d *Decide upon the best method to provide evidence for these conclusions: sort, filter or search?*

e *Load a word processing program, for example, Word.*

f *Open a new document and also open your data file.*

g *Set out your conclusions in the document.*

h *Copy and paste data from the data file to support your conclusions.*

i *Use graphs from the data file to present the evidence so that it is easy to read and understand.*

Task 3

1 *Work with a partner to write an account of the stages of testing a hypothesis by using a data file.*

Think about all of the stages of work through this module:
- *working out a hypothesis*
- *deciding on the data that is needed to test a hypothesis*
- *creating questionnaires and gathering the data*
- *creating a database with the data*
- *checking the integrity of the data (for mistakes and gaps)*
- *interrogating the data*
- *drawing conclusions*
- *presenting the evidence.*

2 *Consider where it could be important for you to make judgements about the plausibility of data in the future.*

 ## Skills help

Using a word processor, pages 108–10.

Inserting data and graphs from Excel into a word processor, page 110.

Task 2

*You are to set up a report so that the graphs in the report will automatically update if **variables** in the data file change.*

1 *When creating your report, instead of **Copy and Paste** use **Paste Special** and click on **Paste link** to maintain a link between a graph in your report and the data file.*

2 *Close all the files.*

3 *Re-open your data file and change some of the variables.*

Any graphs you have made in the data file should have changed with the data.

4 *Re-open your report document and the graphs there should also have changed.*

Are girls richer?

To complete Module 5 you are to test out the following hypothesis:
12-year-old girls get more pocket money than 12-year-old boys.

Background

Shopping is a common pursuit for boys and girls. Do the things they buy cost the same?

Brief

In order to test the hypothesis, you will have to conduct a survey amongst 12-year-olds, using a questionnaire. The data that you need to collect will have to cover the full range of 'pocket money'.

Things to think about:

1 Does it matter how often they receive pocket money or is it just the total amount that is important?
2 Does it matter if they get extra money for clothing, clubs, sports equipment?
3 Who should complete the questionnaire? How many responses do you need to make your evidence plausible?

Gather your data using the questionnaire

Create a data file to store the data in such a way that you will be able to use the data to provide evidence for a report.

Use your data file to find out how much pocket money girls and boys get each week, month and year.

Keep your conclusions secret until you publish a report with your findings.

'SSHHH!!'

Produce graphs in the best format to show the data clearly. Will you consider using column or line graphs?

Write a report that gives your conclusions and has supporting evidence.

PUBLISH THE REPORT!

The tasks in this unit use a flat file database which can be created in Excel, so most of the skills you need for this unit can be found in the Skills help section of Module 4.

Software skills

Calculating percentages

A percentage shows what **proportion** of the total a number represents. It is calculated by dividing the number by the total.

Group	Number	Percentage
Green	18	=B2/B10
Brown	47	
Red	29	
Blue	67	
Orange	45	
Pink	21	
Yellow	11	
Purple	56	
Total	=SUM(B2:B9)	

B2 / B10

In order to make the result show as a percentage rather than a number, you need to change the number format of the cell:

1 Click on the cell you want to format.
2 Click on **Format**, **Cells**. The Format Cells dialogue box appears.

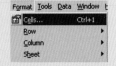

3 Click on the **Number** tab.

4 In the Category window choose Percentage.
5 Choose the number of decimal places you want.
6 Click on **OK**.

Special note: In the example above, if you were going to copy the formula from cell C2 into cells C3 to C9 you would need to make the reference in the formula to cell B10 an **absolute cell reference**, otherwise it would change as you copied the formula down the column. So the formula you would need to type in C2 would be B2/$B$10.

For more information on absolute cell references see page 107.

Group	Number	Percentage
Green	18	=B2/$B$10
Brown	47	=B3/$B$10
Red	29	=B4/$B$10
Blue	67	=B5/$B$10
Orange	45	=B6/$B$10
Pink	21	=B7/$B$10
Yellow	11	=B8/$B$10
Purple	56	=B9/$B$10
Total	=SUM(B2:B9)	=B10/$B$10

Setting up a data structure

A database is made up of a number of records. Each record contains a number of fields. The fields are exactly the same in every record of a database.

Field names. These should be typed across the top of your worksheet as column headings. It is a good idea to make them bold or italic so that they stand out.

Record numbers. These are entered down the left-hand side of your worksheet. Each record should be given a unique number which is never repeated.

When you have set up a table with column and row headings, you can type data into the cells: either numeric or alphanumeric.

The entire column for each field should be formatted according to what data type is in that field.

For help with formatting cells in Excel, including number formats, see page 105.

Record number	First name	Surname	Gender	Age
1	Sarah	Evans	F	12
2	Peter	Smith	M	14
3	John	Brown	M	14

Data analysis skills

Sorting lists

1 Highlight the data you want to sort.
   NB It is very important that you highlight *all* **the data in your database, including the record numbers, before you sort.**
2 Click on **Data**, **Sort**.

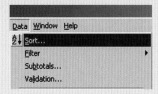

3 Click on the down arrow in the **Sort by** window and choose the first column that you want to sort by.

4 Click either the **Ascending** or **Descending** button.
5 Click on the down arrow in the **Then by** window and choose the second column that you want to sort by.
6 Click either the **Ascending** or **Descending** button.
7 If the data you have highlighted includes field headings then click on the **Header row** button.
8 Click **OK**.

Filtering lists

1 Highlight the data you would like to filter.
2 Click on **Data**, **Filter**, **AutoFilter**. A drop-down menu appears in each column heading.

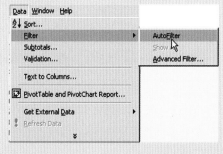

3 Click on the drop-down menu for the column you want to filter. A list of filtering options appears.

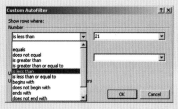

If you want to filter by one thing only:

4 Select it from the list.

If you want to filter by more than one of the things on the list:

5 Click on (**Custom…**) The **Custom AutoFilter** dialog box appears.
6 Click on the top left list arrow to choose the type of filter.
7 Click on the top right list arrow to choose the data list.

8 Enter your second set of selection criteria in the bottom two windows.
9 Click on the **And** button if you want to find only records which match *both* sets of selection criteria.
10 Click on the **Or** button if you want to find all records which match *either* one *or* the other selection criteria.
11 Click on **OK**.
12 Click away to deselect the data and view the filtered data.

Filtering more than one column at a time:

If you filter one column and then do another filter on another column, that is an AND search across both columns. You can carry on filtering as many columns as you want. As you add each new filter the computer will only find the records which match the filter criteria for *all* the filters you have set up.

In this module you will learn about the use and methods of control systems, and how to design them using flowcharts and computer programming. You may already have done some work with control systems and devices in your primary school.

Before you start there are some skills and words that you will need to know. Read about each skill in the boxes below and then decide which of the following statements best describes how you feel about it:

A I am confident that I understand / can do this.
B I think I understand / can do this, but I would like to check.
C I definitely don't know how to do this and I need to learn.

Control system

Control systems are used in everyday items such as pelican crossings, car park barriers, washing machines and video recorders. They are machines containing computer programs which are used to make something happen automatically. **Pixie** and **Roamer** are two devices that you might have used before. You might have written a sequence of commands to move them in a planned way.

Pixie

Roamer

Procedure

A **procedure** is a sequence of instructions that tell a computer to do something. The instructions are very detailed and have to be written in the right order. The software used to run devices such as Pixie and Roamer uses procedures. **LOGO** is a software program that allows you to write procedures.

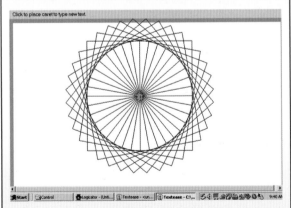

LOGO. This is a programming code that allows you to move items on screen or to draw shapes. You can draw shapes and make patterns by writing the correct series of instructions.

Control interface

Control interfaces are boxes or devices that are connected to a computer for a control system. Different items to be controlled can be attached to the boxes. These are **output devices**. To complete a system, the control interface can also be linked to **sensors** that are called **input devices**.

Output devices. These are the things that are controlled by a control system. Motors, light bulbs, buzzers, water pumps and fans can all be output devices.

Switch. This is a device which is either on or off.

Sensors. These are the devices that send signals to a computer. They are what starts a control system working. Push **switches**, magnetic **switches**, light, heat and sound sensors are examples of sensor input devices.

Program or programme?

A computer runs **programs**.

A television displays **programmes**.

Task

Copy and complete this passage, using the words listed in the box below to fill in the blank.

A control system is used to make something happen .... An example of a control system can be found in a .... or a .... The instructions which tell the system what to do are called .... Control interfaces are boxes or devices that are attached to the computer. Items which are controlled by the system are called .... devices. Examples are .... and .... The control system can also be linked to input devices called .... These give information to the computer about when to start and stop different procedures. Examples of sensors are .... and ....

> **automatically, buzzers, motors, output, pelican crossing, procedures, sensors, sound sensors, switches, video recorder**

Computer control model

A **computer control model** is a program on a computer that simulates a real life event. A model can be set to represent a dangerous situation that people would not want to be in – for example a car that is crashing. Scientists may need to know what happens in such an event and can use a control model to take the place of a person.

Unit 8.1
Control systems in everyday life

In this unit you are going to make a **control system** by writing sets of instructions to control a car park barrier. You will learn about **procedures** and repeated processes.

Control technology

Control technology is the use of control systems to switch **output devices** on and off in a precise sequence, or in response to an **input device** like a light, sound, temperature or movement sensor.

Control systems

Control systems exist all around us. The system could be:

- an automatic door
- an escalator that starts when someone walks onto it
- an automatic watering system in a greenhouse
- a washing machine
- a fire alarm system.

In each case these control systems make use of electronic circuits containing chips that store a control program. **Programmers** create programs on a computer and then download them onto a chip. The chip is then inserted into an electronic circuit.

It is very important to program events in the right order or chaos can occur.

A control system in everday life.

▶ *Skills help*

Understanding computer control systems, pages 157–158.

Writing control procedures

You need to know a few words about systems before you can write instructions:

procedure   a sequence of instructions

automatic   something that happens without the help of a human being

program   a set of instructions for a computer.

Now look at Task 1. For this first task you are going to write a **sequence of instructions**, or a procedure, for someone who has never ridden a bike before to follow.

Automated systems

Control systems can make life easier and sometimes improve our lives. Would you be happy to take temperature readings every five minutes and decide whether to switch on a refrigerator to keep food stocks cool? As this is a **repeated process**, an **automatic** system to **monitor** temperature would be better.

However, life may not always be suited to automated systems. For example, would you like a programmed robot to perform a surgical operation on you? It is important to weigh up the situations that suit automation and those that do not.

Task 1

Look at **Resource 6.1 Bikes**.

1 What are the stages of riding a bike?

2 Write a set of instructions for how to ride a bike. Remember, the person has never ridden a bike before.

3 Check your instructions by watching the video again. Are they in the right order?

'No! I've told you before. On a Saturday I don't have to get up at 7 o'clock!'

Task 2

Look at **Resource 6.1 Automation**.

1 List five advantages of using automation in our everyday lives.

2 List five disadvantages of automation.

Control interface

A control interface is a box that allows a computer to control and power output devices. It can also detect the state of input devices and send that information to the computer.

Input/output devices

Control systems usually depend on an input to start, stop or **modify** the process. A computer will be able to sense when an input device is on or off and will respond by turning output devices on or off.

There are two types of input from an input device such as a switch or a sensor. These are:

digital input   where the input device is on or off, such as a light switch

analogue input   where a range of values are sent to the computer from devices such as sensors for temperature, light and sound.

It is often necessary to measure analogue input over a long period of time, at regular intervals. For example, in a central heating system the room temperature is measured continuously and the system is switched on or off depending on the room temperature at any time.

Sometimes it is useful to collect data from a sensor to look at, as well as to control a system. This is called **data logging**. See pages 164–5 for more information on this.

Module Task

The Module Task helps you to learn about the different methods of controlling systems. Control systems are all about getting things in the right order.

 Look at **Resource 6.1 Barrier 1** and **Resource 6 Flowchart outline**.

a What happens when the car reaches the barrier?

b Record the sequence of events after the car reaches the barrier.

c Annotate your work to show which elements are output devices and which involve input devices.

 Skills help

Understanding input and output devices, pages 157–8.

Task 3

 Look at **Resource 6.1 Barrier 2**.

This shows a different type of control system in use at a car park.

1 Write down the sequence of events, starting with a car approaching the barrier.
- What triggers the barrier to rise?
- What triggers the barrier to lower?

2 What additional safety devices do you think are incorporated into the system?

3 What additional features could you add to the control system to improve it? List the input and output devices that you would use.

Task 4

 Look at **Resource 6.1 Input**.

Here are some common input devices:

temperature sensor
light sensor
sound sensor
movement sensor
rotation sensor
magnetic switch
push switch
pressure mat
oxygen sensor

For each one, write down how you think it could be used in a control system.

Manual or automatic?

Control systems have many advantages. They can:
- be left running all the time, unlike people who need to rest
- be left alone to run without monitoring by a person
- be programmed to do dull, boring repetitive processes that people would not want to do
- be very reliable and eliminate human error
- be cheaper than employing people.

However, there are also some issues to consider.
- Installing an automated system may mean that some people lose their jobs.
- It is possible to make very complex control programs that can, for example, adapt to new situations or tell you when they are going wrong. However, the cost of making such a system might be so high that employing a person is cheaper.

'But I just don't feel like work today!'

Flowcharts

A **flowchart** is a sequence of instructions used to mimic, or **simulate**, a control program. It is used to plan out how a program should work. For example, if you were going to program a robot to do something, you would have to think about all of the actions it needs to take while it's working and all the possible problems that might occur.

Task 1

1 List three activities that are best suited to automatic control systems.

2 List three that are best done by people.

3 Give reasons why in each case.

You would want to make the program as **efficient** as possible so that no effort would be wasted. An efficient program uses the least possible number of instructions or steps to achieve what is required.

Programmers use several ways to plan their control programs and a flowchart is one of them.

Each program must have a **start** symbol at the beginning and a **stop** symbol at the end of the program.

The state of a device is shown using the **input** and **output** symbols for example, 'lamp off'.

When we want something to happen, like a lamp to be turned on, then we use a **process** symbol to give the instruction 'Turn on lamp'.

When we want to allow more than one possible outcome, depending on what the input is, then we use a **decision** symbol. A decision can only have two possible answers, yes or no. For example, 'Do you want milk?' not 'How many sugars would you like?'

A computer program can be very long and parts of the program repeated several times. The parts that are repeated can be made into small programs inside the big program. These are called **subroutines**. A subroutine is a small group of instructions that can be called up by the **main program** at any time. For example, a program for a lift would include the commands, 'Open door and make sound when door opens'. As this would happen on each floor it would make sense to make these commands a subroutine.

A flowchart helps to:
• separate a problem into its parts
• make sure the instructions are in the right order.

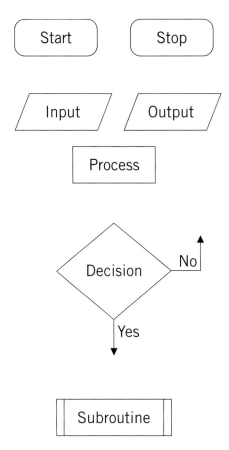

Task 2

A set of instructions to tell someone how to chew gum may look like this:

 Look at **Resource 6.2 Gum flowchart**, which was created in Flowol.

1 Will this flowchart work? Are the instructions correct? Is it complete?

2 Make any additions and alterations that improve the instructions.

 3 Use **Resource 6 Flowchart outline** to write out your new improved flowchart.

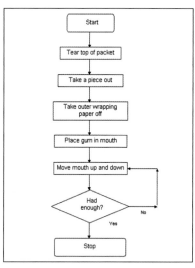

Start

Tear top of packet

Take a piece out

Take outer wrapping paper off

Place gum in mouth

Move mouth up and down

Had enough?   No

Yes

Stop

Module Task

Creating a control system is all about getting things in the right order and writing a good sequence of instructions. In this task you are going to write instructions to make a piece of toast.

a What would the processes of making a piece of toast be?

b What would the control instructions be?

c What symbols represent the process?

d Are any of the processes going to be subroutines?

e Write your sequence of instructions. Discuss these with a partner.

f Is their solution very different to yours?

g Is it more efficient?

 Skills help

Understanding flowcharts, page 158.

Task 3

 Look at **Resource 6.2 Buggy** and **Resource 6 Flowchart outline**.

You are to plan a control program to drive this buggy. The buggy has two motors, one to drive each wheel.

You need the program to:
● drive the buggy forward for 2 seconds
● stop and wait for 1 second
● turn through a quarter of a turn (90 degrees to the right or left)
● drive the buggy forward for 2 seconds and stop.

Draw up a simple flowchart or set of instructions for this program.

Unit 6.3

Using a sensor as a switch in a control model

In this unit you will learn how to create a set of instructions to control an output device in response to physical data that has been recorded by a sensor.

Loop of life!

Does this list of activities on the right look familiar? It is an example of a **loop**.

This loop looks like the life of a couch potato! Generally most of us vary from a basic routine so our lives could not be shown as a loop, because each day is different in some way.

Loops are used when we need to repeat an action or to jump to another action. There are many places in our everyday lives where we come into contact with control systems that have been programmed with **subroutines** and loops. A loop provides a way of monitoring, or constantly checking and rechecking, a system.

1	Get up
2	Eat
3	Go to school
4	Eat
5	Go home
6	Eat
7	Do homework
8	Eat
9	Watch TV or see friends
10	Eat
11	Go to bed

The equipment in this premature baby unit depends on loops to constantly check the progress of the baby.

Look at **Resource 6.3 Crossing**.

1 Create a flowchart that simulates what happens when somebody makes use of a pelican crossing to cross a road.

- What are the stages or sequence of events?
- How is it controlled?
- How is it automated?

2 Your flowchart will need to make use of at least one loop. Think about what it is that causes the lights to turn red.

Input devices for safety and if… then… conditions

Automated systems make use of input devices. Input devices can be used to make things safe by checking and rechecking the system is working correctly.

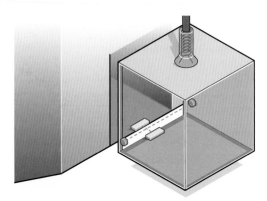

This picture shows a lift with a light sensor to ensure no one is standing in the door before it closes. The program checks '**if** the light beam is broken **then** do not shut the door'. Above the lift there is a stress sensor, which checks that the load is not over the recommended weight. There is also a sensor to make sure the lift is in the correct position against the floor level before the doors open. In each case the lift is programmed to check '**if… then…**'

1 Work with a partner to write a sequence of instructions for a lift that goes up and down between three floors.

2 What is the most efficient way for the lift to work?

3 Should it go up and down all the way?

4 How does it know which floor to go to next?

5 What safety checks have to happen before the lift can start or stop?

6 Show on your sequence where loops or subroutines could be programmed.

 As a safety feature all control systems have to be left in a safe state if they fail. This makes sure the system does not harm people.

 Skills help

Understanding 'If… then…', page 158.

Module Task

This Module Task builds on your knowledge of the methods used in control systems by studying one that includes a sensor to check for safety.

 Look at **Resource 6.3 Car safety**.

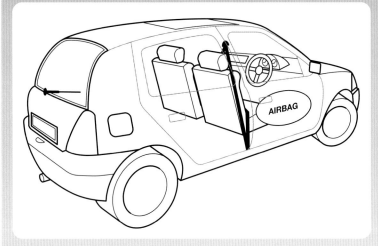

a List ten sensors that could be used on a car. You might use the same type of sensor more than once for different reasons.

b State how you think the sensors increase the safety of the car.

c Add a new safety feature of your own to do one of the following things:
- to help with parking
- to turn on hazard lights in fog
- to tell when the car needs washing.

  i What type of sensor would be needed for your safety feature?
  ii What type of warning would be provided to the driver?

d Create the flowchart that would simulate the computer program required to operate your safety feature.

Task 3

Take your chosen safety feature for the Module Task a stage further.

1 Develop your flowchart to include output devices that would be turned off until a safety sensor indicates it is safe. For example, 'If the car door is open, then do not allow the engine to start.'

Task 4

Most accidents occur in the home. The most dangerous place in the home is the kitchen.

1 Which are the potentially dangerous areas in a kitchen?

2 Choose one of these.

3 Design a control system to make it safer.

4 Create a flowchart to demonstrate how it would work.

Unit 6.4
Creating and testing control systems

Putting programs together

A control system may contain several safety devices. Most systems continually have to check the state of each sensor by using loops. This means that there are several programs running at the same time.

A modern car has many safety features, which are all checked continually. The flowcharts for each of these safety features are very similar. Each contains a loop consisting of signals from input sensors and one or more outputs.

Task 1

 Look at **Resource 6.4 Automated room**.

This room could be fully automated so Ben need never leave his seat.

The three flowcharts shown will:
- *turn the fan on if the temperature goes above 26 °C.*
- *turn the fire on when the temperature drops below 26 °C*
- *operate lights and close curtains*

1 *How can you improve the model and make a more efficient system by merging Examples 1 and 2?*

2 *Add in two more control devices to refine the system and make Ben's life even easier!*

Control programs

Different companies write their own programs for use with computer interface boxes. Examples of control programs are Flowol, LEGO RCX and Logicator.

▶ *Skills help*

Using control commands for the main control programs, pages 159–63.

Module Task

This Module Task builds on your knowledge of control systems by studying one that uses parallel processing of several security sensors. It will ask you to set up a computer model of your own design in a control program.

By special command!

The Queen has decided to update security at her castles and at the same time reduce the number of Beefeaters that she needs.

She wants to be able to safely raise the drawbridge, lower the portcullis and turn the gas ring on to heat the boiling oil, and sound a warning alarm to raise the Horse Guards.

*a Look at **Resource 6.4 Castle map**. Think about the layout of the castle. Where would you add sensors to make sure that the motors operating the systems stop at the right time?*

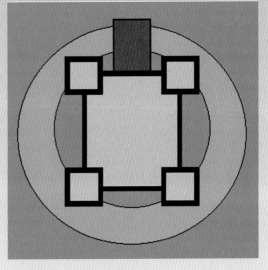

b What sort of sensors would you need? Switches, light sensors?

c Make notes on your layout to show where the sensors would go.

d Draw a flowchart for each sensor.

e Write a series of programs that would activate the security systems that the Queen wants.

Project teams

Programmers often have to work on very big programs. These may be too complicated for one programmer, so they form project teams. Each member of the team works on one subroutine, or **subtask**. Now you are going to work with partners as a project team.

 Look at **Resource 6.4 Automated greenhouse**.

In this task you should work in a team with two or three other people.

1 *As a team, write a list of the physical conditions a gardener might want to monitor in a greenhouse that is used for growing flowers. Think about:*
   ● *what makes plants grow?*
   ● *what would be the very best growing conditions?*
   ● *how could the gardener grow flowers all through the year?*

2 *State the sensor that could be used for each of the conditions – describe the function it carries out if you do not know the technical name.*

3 *Each team member is responsible for creating the flowchart and writing the program to control one of these conditions.*

4 *Bring all of the programs together and check each of the flowcharts.*

5 *Can you work out how they could be combined into one control program?*

This way of working is exactly how programs are developed in industry. Very rarely does one person write a program, it is always a team effort.

Testing systems

Systems always have to be tested to check that they work in the way expected. The testing process should make sure that:
• every part of program works
• the program handles information from input devices correctly
• the program reports if the system is faulty in some way.

In the Module Task, the Queen's security system needed a series of programs. This is not efficient. Write a program that will bring together the programs from the Module Task so that the Queen can control the security system at the touch of a single button. Use your knowledge of flowcharts, loops and parallel processing.

Today many people are health-conscious and go to gyms or take regular exercise.

1 *Think of the ways you could check to see how healthy you are.*

2 *What conditions would you measure? List as many as you can.*

3 *Create a flowchart to show how a computer program could be used to monitor one of the conditions from your list.*

Unit | 6.5

Creating an efficient system to monitor an event

In this unit you are going to learn how to make a control program more efficient.

Merging procedures, subroutines and subtasks

A **procedure**, **subroutine** or **subtask** consist of a small group of instructions that are called up by the **main program**.

Think about a production line. There are lots of little jobs going on before the finished product comes off the end of the line. These little jobs are all subtasks and form part of the whole system.

Production lines involve lots of subroutines.

There are always several solutions to a programming problem. However, the best solution is usually the shortest program. The shorter the program the quicker it usually works and it saves you time!

The following example programs all do the same thing; they flash the amber light several times.

Illustration 1

This program requires four lines of programming for each flash. Very hard work!

Illustration 2

This program uses a subroutine that contains those four lines. However, we have to enter one line for each flash.

Illustration 3

In this solution, we only have to change the value of A to determine how many times we want the light to flash.

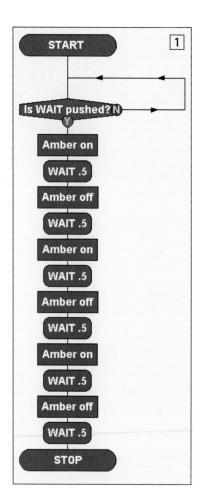

START
Is WAIT pushed? N
Amber on
WAIT .5
Amber off
WAIT .5
Amber on
WAIT .5
Amber off
WAIT .5
Amber on
WAIT .5
Amber off
WAIT .5
STOP

Task 1

Watch **Resource 6.3 Crossing**, then look at Resource **6.5 Pelican Crossing 1** which was created in RM Logicator.

1 Which commands are repeated?

2 How many times is each command repeated?

Look at **Resources 6.5 Pelican Crossing 2** and **3**.

3 How many parts are there to each program?

4 Describe the two different solutions to the same problem.

5 Which one is the best and why?

It is important to be precise when programming commands. For instance, a rocket might miss its target if the program commands are not 100% accurate.

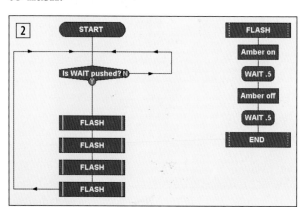

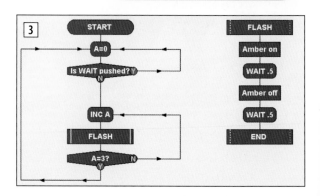

Module Task

 Look at **Resource 6.5 Control commands**.

Use all your knowledge on writing instructions for control systems to make this buggy move. It has two motors, one to drive each wheel. To move forward, both motors need to be turning in the same direction.

Working with a partner, write a set of subroutines to control a variety of buggy movements.

a *Write commands or a group of commands for each of these actions:*
- *drive forward*
- *drive backwards*
- *turn right a quarter of a turn*
- *turn left a quarter of a turn*
- *stop*
- *move forward fast*
- *move forward slow*
- *spin for 1 second.*

b *Use some of these subroutines to create a program to drive the buggy in a square journey. It is hard to get a perfect square as the buggy motors often work at different speeds.*

c *Write down a new journey that your partner will have to program. Think about:*
- *how far it should go*
- *for how long*
- *in which direction*
- *how many times.*

 Skills help

Sample programs, see **Resource 6.5 Control commands**.

Task 2

A new version of the buggy from the Module Task is to be designed. It will have push sensors on the front and back.

1 *Write additional subroutines that will turn all the motors off if the buggy hits a wall.*

2 *Develop the subroutines to create a program that will:*
- *reverse the buggy*
- *turn a bit when it hits the wall.*

Task 3

You are to program a microwave oven. Write a set of instructions that would do the following:
- *set timer for 60 seconds*
- *turn turntable on*
- *switch microwave on*
- *turntable to turn one way for 10 seconds, then the other way for 10 seconds*
- *keep doing this until time has elapsed*
- *turn off microwave*
- *beeper to sound 5 times.*

Jewel show

To complete Module 6 you are to model a control system.

Background

A valuable jewel is to be put on show to the public.
It is about the size of an egg and weighs 130 grams.

Brief

You have just been asked to design an alarm system to protect the jewel.

The container for the jewel and the security system need to work together.

Sketch out some ideas for a container that includes the security system.

Your system should make use of up to five sensors as you don't know how a thief might attempt to get at the jewel!

1 What shape should the container be?
2 Where would sensors have to be placed?
3 How would they protect it?
4 Where would the container be placed? Remember it has to be on public view.

Mark all of the sensors that you would use on your sketch.

Create a flowchart showing a control program that makes use of the sensors.

1 Will your program use parallel processing?
2 Will there be any subtasks running in the program?
3 What safety features should you include so that the system works efficiently? It would not be efficient if alarms went off when anybody went close to it!

Remember

Input   A signal sent from a sensor to the computer

Process   The computer interprets the information from the signal

Output   The computer responds by turning one or more output devices on or off

Computer control system

A computer control system has three stages:

Input. This is when a computer receives a signal that triggers something to happen. This comes from a sensor or input device.

Process. This happens when the computer receives the signal and does something. This could be to do a calculation or to send a signal to an output device.

Output. This is when something happens as a result of the process. This could be to start a motor or turn a heater on or off.

Components of a computer control system

Computer

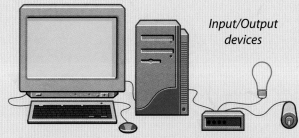

Input/Output devices

Control Interface Box

Sometimes these separate parts cannot be seen as they are built into the device or central system. Think about a washing machine:

- The input is the switch, both at the socket and on the machine itself.
- The computer bit is the circuit board inside the machine that works out which wash cycle to run from the settings and the switches.
- The output is the motor that makes the pump work or opens a valve to let water in.

Devices

Input devices

Sensors are input devices. There are many types of sensor that can be used:

Touch sensors – a pressure mat is a good example of a touch sensor. When you walk across a pressure mat a signal is sent to the computer. If it is part of an alarm system, the alarm would then sound as a response to the signal from the computer.

Light sensors – sense the amount and/or colour of light given off by objects. Robots used in big stock control warehouses are programmed to follow coloured lines leading to different stock areas. They sense the colour line that they are programmed to follow.

Heat sensors – sense temperature and can be used to control the heat in houses, offices or in production lines where heat levels have to be kept the same.

Sound sensors – sense sounds of any type. They can be set to pick up only a particular range of loud sounds, for example if machinery noise gets above a set level, or they can be set to be triggered by the tiniest noise.

Humidity sensors – sense the amount of moisture in the air. They are used in swimming pools or greenhouses.

Radio wave sensors – sense radio waves. They are used by the police in speed trap cameras: the device bounces radio waves off moving objects and the sensor detects them.

Smoke sensors – used in houses, offices, hospitals, hotels and other public places, to detect smoke in the air. They often take readings of how much carbon there is present.

Control interface box

An interface box provides a link between the sensors, the output devices and the computer. Sensors are attached to the interface at one end of a system. The interface may be attached to several sensors at the same time, each one set to have a different role in the system.

Output devices

Output devices do something in response to a signal from the computer. They will perform in the way that the program has been written. They might turn on for a short or long period of time. They might go slowly or very fast.

Motors – motors are a common type of output device because they can drive lots of things. For example, a motor can be used to open a window, lift a barrier or run a fan.

Sounds – bells, buzzers and other sounds can be output devices. In an alarm system, bells and buzzers are triggered by a signal from a computer.

Lights – lights can be turned on by a signal from a computer program. When you press the button at a pelican crossing you are sending a signal to the computer. The computer then processes the information and sends a signal to change the lights to red. This allows you to cross the road. The lights change back again after a time and the whole cycle will be run again when someone else presses the button.

Flowcharts

Flowcharts are really a way of telling a story. They all have to **Start** and **Stop**. They all have **processes** that happen and **decisions** that have to be made.

Programmers use symbols to help them to work out the stages and processes that are needed in a system. They piece the instructions or decisions together to form a flowchart. They create small

programs in the same way. These are called **subroutines** or **subtasks**.

Programmers work out the sequence of commands that are needed to make a program work. They use the symbols to create the program. They join the symbols with lines to show the **FLOW** of information. They put arrows on the lines to show the direction of the flow.

If… then…

Many control systems contain decisions which have to be made at various stages of the program. For example:

> How long should a motor run?
>
> How long should a buzzer sound?

Programmers have either to decide and program in how long to let things go on for, or they have to set **conditions**: **IF** a certain thing happens **THEN** turn the buzzer off. These types of decisions are shown in a **decision box** on a flowchart. The answer in a decision box always has to be **YES** or **NO**. Maybe is just not good enough!

Control commands

You may come across many different types of control programs in practical lessons such as Design and Technology, for example PIC Logicator, PICAXE and Co-Co.

There are three main control programs used in ICT in schools lessons.
These are:

- LEGO RCX
- Flowol
- Logicator.

Each program works differently so you need to check with your teacher which one you are using. You will either drag and drop the icons into a flowchart, or create a flowchart from the symbols already in the program.

The following commands on pages 161 to 166 are the ones that you will need to use to program devices or set up computer models on a computer.

Using LEGO* RCX

Output	LEGO RCX	
Motor		Turn motor connected to A on
Lamp		Turn lamp connected to A on
Speaker		Play a tune
Wait		Wait for 1 second before you go on to the next command
Start		Start of program
End		End of program
Wait – until		Wait until switch 1 has been pushed before you go on to next command

Loops

Loop

Flash a light for 1 second

Parallel processing

If… then…

If input 1 is pressed, then motor goes forward; if input 2 is pressed, then motor goes backward

Flash the light on and off 5 times

LEGO* is a trademark of the LEGO Group, used here with special permission.

Using Flowol

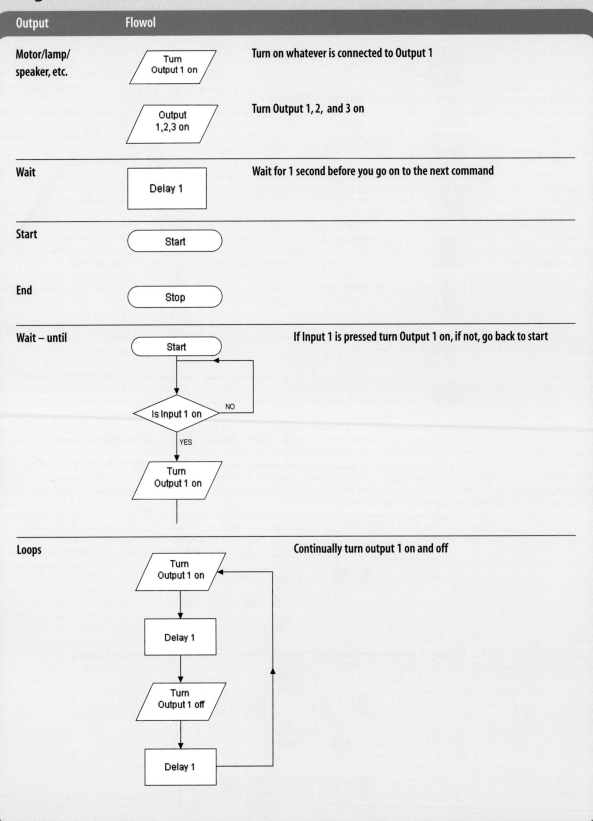

Output	Flowol	
Motor/lamp/ speaker, etc.	Turn Output 1 on	Turn on whatever is connected to Output 1
	Output 1,2,3 on	Turn Output 1, 2, and 3 on
Wait	Delay 1	Wait for 1 second before you go on to the next command
Start	Start	
End	Stop	
Wait – until	Start · Is Input 1 on (NO / YES) · Turn Output 1 on	If Input 1 is pressed turn Output 1 on, if not, go back to start
Loops	Turn Output 1 on · Delay 1 · Turn Output 1 off · Delay 1	Continually turn output 1 on and off

Output   **Flowol**

Parallel processing

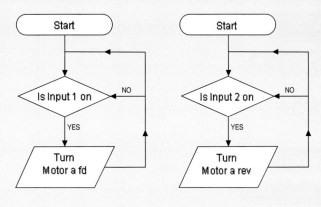

If... then...   If input 1 is pressed, then motor goes forward; if input 2 is pressed, then motor goes backward

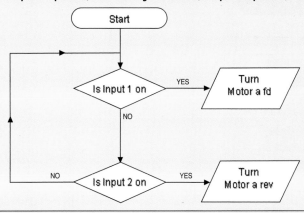

Flash the light on and off 5 times

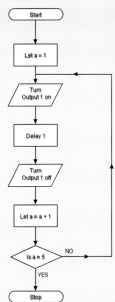

Using Logicator

Output	Logicator
Motor	Ouput 1 on
Lamp/Speaker	Turn on 1, 2 ,3
Wait	WAIT 1
Start	START
End	STOP
Wait – until	

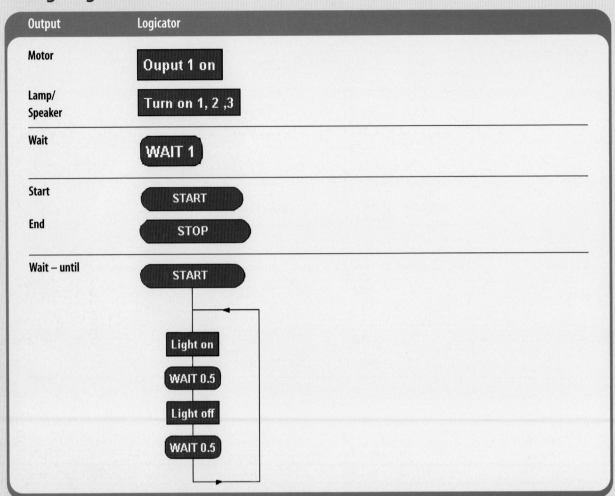

Output	Logicator
Loops	

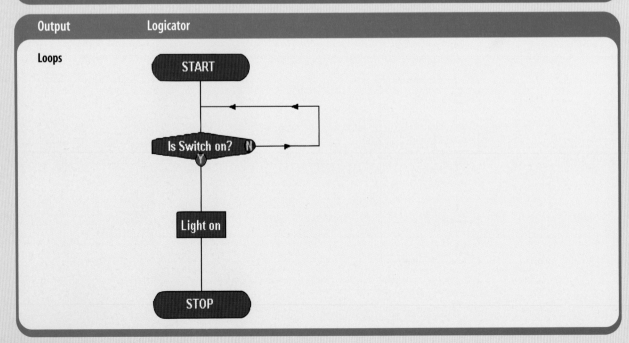

Parallel processing   Not available

If... then...   If input 1 is pressed, then motor goes forward; if input 2 is pressed, then motor goes backward

Parallel processing   Not available

Flash the light on and off 5 times

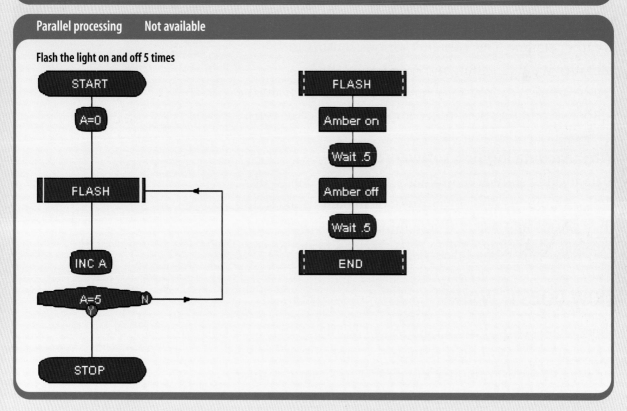

Introduction to data logging

What is data logging?

Sometimes it is useful to capture and measure data from a sensor. This is called **data logging**. You may have done experiments in science using data logging software – for example, measuring how long it takes a liquid to cool or heat up. Another piece of data logging equipment which you may have come across is a weather station. This contains various sensors to measure wind direction and speed, rainfall, temperature, etc. You may have looked at data from the school weather station in geography or science lessons.

A weather station

Why use data logging software?

Data logging software automates the measurement of data. Computers do not get tired, or make mistakes, and they can go into places where humans could not – for example, the inside of an engine, or deep in the ocean.

How does it work?

In order to capture the data a sensor is attached to a computer. The computer records the measurement from the sensor at regular intervals. The length of time between each measurement is called the **logging interval**. The total length of time during which measurements are made is called the **logging period**.

The length of both of these depends on what is being measured and why. Here are two examples:

1 A health and safety inspector wants to know about noise levels in a factory. A sound sensor is used. As the factory works in shifts, seven days a week, the logging period is set for a whole week.

The logging interval is every half an hour because noise levels do not change very quickly.

2 Your science teacher has asked you to set up an experiment to measure how much oxygen is produced by a plant over a period of time. The oxygen is produced quite quickly so the measurements need to be taken every few seconds, over a period of about 2 hours.

Setting up a data logging experiment

Care needs to be taken when setting up the data logging equipment to ensure that the data gathered will answer the questions you want to ask and that it will not be misleading. For example, if you put a sound sensor right next to the noisiest machine in the factory it might give a false idea of how noisy the whole factory was. In this case it might be a good idea to have more than one sensor and place them in different parts of the factory.

What happens to the data after it is logged?

Data which has been logged is **numeric**. A useful tool for analysing this kind of data is a spreadsheet. Usually the data is taken out of the data logging software and **imported** into a spreadsheet. Once it is there it can be sorted or filtered, calculations can be performed on it and the results can be displayed in charts and graphs. Patterns can be seen and conclusions drawn.

Does this sound familiar? It should do, because the skills and techniques used to analyse data from data logging software are the same as those you have learnt in Modules 4 and 5. The only difference is the method by which the data was obtained in the first place.

Task

 Look at **Resource Pondweed 1**.
It shows some real data collected from a science experiment measuring the amount of oxygen produced by pondweed.

1 How easy is it to get information from the data in the table?

2 Make a graph from the data (ask your teacher about what type of graph would be best to use).

3 What information can you get now from the data? Can you draw any conclusions from the experiment?

Extension question

4 How could you alter the presentation of the data in order to make the information clearer in the graph?

Glossary

Absolute cell reference	A cell reference which does not change when cell contents are moved. Indicated by a $ sign in front of each part of the cell reference, e.g. $B$2
Accurate	Containing no errors
Acquire	To obtain an image using a digital camera or scanner (also called capturing an image)
Address (website)	Text that is entered in a browser to go to a website
Alphanumeric	Containing text and numbers, e.g. 1234AZ. A postcode is alphanumeric
Animate	To make move, bring to life
Annotate	To add notes to a printout or screenshot to explain something
Audience	The people who will look at or use something
Automate	To make something work without human help
Bar chart	A chart, similar to a graph, showing data values in horizontal rectangles or bars
Biased	Showing favour to one point of view
Bitmapped graphic (bmp file)	An image stored as a collection of coloured dots (pixels)
Browse	To look through lists of files, images, clip art or web pages
Bullet point	Symbol, usually a dot or small square, put at the beginning of a line of text
Capture	To obtain an image from a scanner or camera (also called acquiring an image)
Cell	The smallest part of a spreadsheet or database table. It is the 'box' that an individual piece of data is entered into
Cell reference	The address which tells you where a cell is, using the column letters and row numbers, e.g. A1, C12
Classify	To group similar types of things together, e.g. oranges, apples and pears are classified as fruits
Column chart	A chart, similar to a graph, showing data values in vertical rectangles or bars
Control	To make something happen
Copyright	Protected by law from unauthorised copying
Corporate image	An image used to represent a company or organisation
Criteria	The standards by which something can be judged
Criterion	A standard by which something can be judged
Crop	To hide part of an image to change the way the image looks
Cut	To remove text or data from a file
Data	Items which are stored or processed by a computer, e.g. numbers, text or images
Data structure	The way data is set up in a computer so that it can be used
Data type	In a database system, data type means whether a piece of data is text, numeric or alphanumeric
Database	A collection of data stored in an organised way on a computer
Database software	A computer program used to store, organise and interrogate a database
Decision	A choice made from various options available
Design brief	A guide to tell someone what they have to create
Desktop publishing (DTP)	Software used to create documents such as leaflets

Digital camera	A camera that does not use film, but creates electronic images
Document	Letters, leaflets, advertisements and reports are all examples of documents
Download	To store a file or image on a computer that is taken from another source, such as the Internet
dpi (dots per inch)	The number of dots or pixels which make up one square inch of a picture. dpi measures the quality of an image: the more dots per inch, the higher the quality of the image
Draft	A rough copy of something before the final copy is created
Drag and drop	To move text or images by holding down the left mouse button and moving it to a new place in a document
Effective	Something is effective if it does the job it was intended to do
Efficient	Something is efficient if it works with the least possible waste of time or effort
Evaluate	To judge how well something worked or is working
Field	The part of a database that holds a single item of data, such as Age or Height
Fitness for purpose	Whether a document, image or presentation matches the audience that it is being developed for
Flowchart	A way of showing the stages and processes to make something happen, including decisions, calculations and outcome of actions
Font	A particular typeface, such as Arial or Times New Roman
Font attributes	The way that a font looks, e.g. its style, size, whether it is bold, italic or underlined
Format	The way in which data is displayed or stored
Formula	The way in which a calculation is shown in a spreadsheet, e.g. =A2+B2
Graphics	The use, creation or changing of pictures, images and shapes on a computer
Heading	Title at the head of a document or presentation slide
Hits	Visits to a website. Every time someone visits a website, the website registers a 'hit'
Home page	The first web page that you see when you visit a website
Hyperlink	A link between two places. The link could be between web pages, websites, documents, images or a mixture of any of these
Hypothesis	An idea that is put forward in order to test whether or not it is true
'if ... then ...'	A set of conditions that can make something happen, e.g. 'if I am thirsty then I will have a drink'
Image	A picture, drawing or photograph, when they are used on a computer
Import	To bring in data or images from one computer program into another
Index	An alphabetical list of items of information
Information source	Places to find information, such as books, CDs or the Internet
Input	Something which goes into a computer program. This could be data or a signal in a control sequence
Input device	Hardware which is used to input data into a computer, e.g. a keyboard or a light sensor
Internet	A gigantic network of computers from all around the world linked through different types of connections, such as telephone lines, cable, microwave, satellite and radio technology
Interrogate	To ask questions in order to get information. A database can be interrogated
Judge	To decide whether something is good, working well or could be improved
Label	A name which identifies an item of data in a spreadsheet
Layering	To place items such as images and text on top of one another in a document

Layout	The way images, text or data are put together and presented in a document
Line graph	A set of data plotted as points on an X axis and a Y axis
Locate	To find the place where information is being held
Log on	To access a computer network
Logic	A structured way of thinking in different stages in order to get a final result
Logo	A badge, symbol or graphic used to represent a company
Loop	A section of a flowchart which is repeated
Menu	A list of items to choose from
Microphone	A device through which sounds can be recorded
Model	A software application, such as a spreadsheet, that is used to represent a real-life situation
Multimedia	Involving the use of text, sound and graphics, and possibly video or animation
Network	A number of computers linked together in order to share software and devices such as printers
Numeric	Made up of numbers only (no text)
Opinion	An attitude or viewpoint
Opinion poll	A way of asking for and recording lots of people's opinions
Origin	Where something comes from
Output	What happens at the end of a computer program, e.g. a bell ringing in an alarm system, a printout of a document
Output device	Hardware that can output data in some form, e.g. the bell, the printer
Paste	To place data that has been cut or copied from somewhere else
Pie chart	A way of presenting data so that it looks like a pie cut up into different sized slices
Plausible	Something is plausible if it can be easily believed
Precise	Exact
Predict	To state what might happen
Presentation software	Software that combines text, colours and images to get a message across to an audience
Procedure	Instructions to a computer to do something, e.g. to carry out a calculation
Process	A computer actually doing something, e.g. carrying out a calculation
Program	A series of instructions to make something happen
Programmer	Someone who writes computer programs
Purpose	The reason for making something appear as it does or happen in a certain way
Query	A set of questions to tell a computer to look for something in a database
Questionnaire	A document with a series of questions that could be used to test a hypothesis
Record	A complete set of data about one person or item, e.g. a person's medical history stored in a database
Refine	To improve something to make it more effective or efficient
Relative cell reference	A cell reference used in a formula. If the formula is moved, the cell reference changes to match the new position. For example, the formula B2+C2 would become B3+C3 if it was moved to the next row down
Reliable	Something that is safe and can be trusted
Representative sample	A small group of people chosen to answer a questionnaire because they are very similar to the whole population. So if a reseacher wanted to get the opinion of all teenagers, they might choose a sample of 2000 people aged 13–19, evenly split between boys and girls, and taken from all parts of the country

Sample	A small selection taken from a big group
Sample composition	The types of people or items which make up a sample
Sample size	The number of items or people in a sample
Scanner	Input device for photographs or images
Search	To find data or files on a computer or the Internet
Search engine	A piece of software that allows you to type in words connected with the data that you want to find, in order to find it
Search method	How to go about finding information, e.g. using the Internet or visiting a library
Sensor	An input device which detects physical events and converts them into an electrical signal which can be received by a computer
Shared area	Area on a computer network where files can be stored and accessed by more than one computer
Simulate	To pretend to carry out actions or calculations that could happen in a real-life situation
Sort	To put into an order, e.g. to sort into alphabetical order
Speaker	A device needed to hear recorded sound
Start	An instruction used at the beginning of a control program
Stop	An instruction used at the end of a control program
Style	One of the different attributes for a font, e.g. bold, underlined, italic
Subheading	Information or a title that comes underneath the main title
Subroutine	A small program (series of instructions) that is written within a program
Subtask	An instruction to carry out an action within a subroutine
Survey	Research done in order to find out people's opinions on a specific subject
Switch	An input device which is either on or off
System (i)	An organised way of working
System (ii)	A set of connected things or parts which work together to produce something
Table	A way of showing data in rows and columns
Template	A file or document set up to be used again and again without change, e.g. an order form
Uniform resource locator (URL)	The unique address of a website, e.g. http://www.heinemann.co.uk is the URL of Heinemann Publishers
Value	A numeric amount, e.g. 12.5 or £4000
Variable	Something that can be changed in a model in order to see what effect it has
Vector graphic	An image stored as a collection of lines and shapes, e.g. clip art
Viewpoint	A person's opinion; the way they see things
Voice-over	Words which are recorded and added to a presentation or animation in order to give more information
Web browser	Software used to access the World Wide Web
Web page	A single page of a website
Website	All of the web pages to do with one subject and one company, linked together
White space	The areas in a document where there is nothing: no images, no text and no border
World Wide Web (www)	The multimedia information that is stored on the Internet